EXPLORING
ANCIENT
CIVILIZATIONS

6

Indus Valley – Marduk

Marshall Cavendish

Marshall Cavendish
99 White Plains Road
Tarrytown, New York 10591-9001

www.marshallcavendish.com

Consultants: Daud Ali, School of Oriental and African
Studies, University of London; Michael Brett, School
of Oriental and African Studies, London; John
Chinnery, School of Oriental and African Studies,
London; Philip de Souza; Joann Fletcher; Anthony
Green; Peter Groff, Department of Philosophy,
Bucknell University; Mark Handley, History
Department, University College London; Anders
Karlsson, School of Oriental and African Studies,
London; Alan Leslie, Glasgow University Archaeology
Research Department; Michael E. Smith, Department
of Anthropology, University at Albany; Matthew
Spriggs, Head of School of Archaeology and
Anthropology, Australian National University

Contributing authors: Richard Balkwill, Richard
Burrows, Peter Chrisp, Richard Dargie, Steve Eddy,
Clive Gifford, Jen Green, Peter Hicks, Robert Hull,
Jonathan Ingoldby, Pat Levy, Steven Maddocks, John
Malam, Saviour Pirotta, Stewart Ross, Sean Sheehan,
Jane Shuter

WHITE-THOMSON PUBLISHING
Editors: Alex Woolf and Kelly Davis
Design: Derek Lee
Cartographer: Peter Bull Design
Picture Research: Glass Onion Pictures
Indexer: Fiona Barr

MARSHALL CAVENDISH
Editor: Thomas McCarthy
Editorial Director: Paul Bernabeo
Production Manager: Michael Esposito

Library of Congress Cataloging-in-Publication Data
Exploring ancient civilizations.
    p. cm.
Includes bibliographical references and indexes.
    ISBN 0-7614-7456-0 (set : alk. paper) -- ISBN 0-7614-7457-9 (v. 1 :
alk. paper) -- ISBN 0-7614-7458-7 (v. 2 : alk. paper) -- ISBN
0-7614-7459-5 (v. 3 : alk. paper) -- ISBN 0-7614-7460-9 (v. 4 : alk.
paper) -- ISBN 0-7614-7461-7 (v. 5 : alk. paper) -- ISBN 0-7614-7462-5
(v. 6 : alk. paper) -- ISBN 0-7614-7463-3 (v. 7 : alk. paper) -- ISBN
0-7614-7464-1 (v. 8 : alk. paper) -- ISBN 0-7614-7465-X (v. 9 : alk.
paper) -- ISBN 0-7614-7466-8 (v. 10 : alk. paper) -- ISBN 0-7614-7467-6
(v. 11 : alk. paper)
    1. Civilization, Ancient--Encyclopedias.
    CB311.E97 2004
    930'.03--dc21

                                    2003041224

ISBN 0-7614-7456-0 (set)
ISBN 0-7614-7462-5 (vol. 6)

Printed and bound in China

07 06 05 04 03 5 4 3 2 1

ILLUSTRATION CREDITS

AKG London: 414 (Vatican, Rome), 416 (Jean-Louis Nou), 419 (Erich Lessing), 421
(Museo Nazionale Romano delle Terme, Rome / Erich Lessing), 425, 428 (Erich Lessing),
430 (Peter Connolly), 431 (AKG Berlin), 435 (National Museum of India, New Delhi /
Jean-Louis Nou), 447 (Jean-Louis Nou), 453 (Bibliothèque Nationale, Paris), 455, 460, 461,
474 (Asiatic Society of Bombay / Jean-Louis Nou), 478 (Musée du Louvre, Paris / Erich
Lessing).
Ancient Art and Architecture: 432, 437, 466, 467.
Australian National University: 458 (Dr Glenn Summerhayes).
Bridgeman Art Library: 406 (National Museum of India, New Delhi), 407 (National
Museum of Karachi, Pakistan), 408 (National Museum of Karachi, Pakistan), 412 (Leeds
Museums and Galleries, UK), 413 (Museum of Fine Arts, Houston / A. C. Arnold
Endowment Fund & McAshan Charitable Trust), 417 (Brooklyn Museum of Art, New
York), 418 (Index), 420 (Agnew & Sons, London), 423 (Kunsthistorisches Museum,
Vienna), 424 (Bonhams, London), 426, 427 (National Gallery of Victoria, Melbourne,
Australia), 429 (Musée de Picardie, Amiens, France), 438 (Musée du Louvre, Paris), 439, 440
(National Archaeological Museum, Athens), 444, 445, 449 (Kunsthistorisches Museum,
Vienna), 459, 462, 463 (National Museum of India, New Delhi), 464 (British Museum,
London), 465 (Museo Archeologico, Florence), 469 (Archaeological Museum, Thessaloniki,
Greece), 470 (Museo Archeologico Nazionale, Naples), 471 (Musée du Louvre, Paris), 472
(Oriental Museum, Durham University, UK), 475 (Fitzwilliam Museum, University of
Cambridge), 476, 477 (Detroit Institute of Arts).
C. M. Dixon: 434, 450.
Robert Harding: 405, 433, 457.
South American Pictures: 452.
Werner Forman Archive: 409 (Iraq Museum, Baghdad), 410 (British Museum, London),
422 (British Museum, London), 443 (History Museum, Kaisyeng, North Korea), 448
(Theresa McCullough Collection, London), 454 (Haiphong Museum, Vietnam), 473.

Contents

Indus Valley

The Indus River valley of northwestern India and Pakistan was the site of one of the world's earliest civilizations, along with China, Egypt, and Mesopotamia. As in Egypt and Mesopotamia, the Indus civilization grew up alongside rivers that flooded regularly; the rivers provided water and rich, fertile soil for farming.

The Indus people were unique among early civilizations for several reasons. There is no evidence that they had kings or a state religion. There are no statues or wall carvings of rulers or gods, no royal tombs, and no obvious temples. Furthermore, there is no evidence of warfare; few weapons have been found, and there are no images of soldiers or of fighting.

All four early civilizations invented writing, but the Indus people's script has never been deciphered. So everything known about this mysterious ancient civilization comes from archaeological evidence.

The Indus Plain
The Indus plain combined the best features of Mesopotamia and Egypt. Unlike the rivers of Mesopotamia, the Indus River flooded at just the right time for planting crops—between June and September. Whereas the Egyptian Nile flowed through a single long, narrow valley, the Indus flowed across a wide plain and several other rivers flowed into it. Thus, a much larger area was available for farming.

The rivers of the Indus plain provided excellent trade routes. Although the civilization is named after the Indus valley, it eventually spread over a much wider area, along the seacoast to the south and with outposts far to the north, one of which has been found at Shortugai in central Asia. In all, the Indus region covered more than 386,000 square miles (1,000,000 km²).

▼ The development of the Indus valley civilization between 3100 and 2000 BCE.

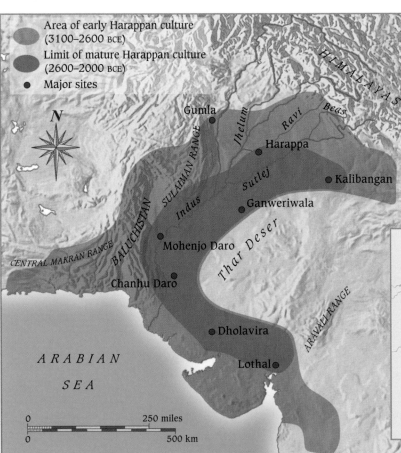

Area of early Harappan culture (3100–2600 BCE)
Limit of mature Harappan culture (2600–2000 BCE)
● Major sites

HIMALAYAS
Gumla
Harappa
Kalibangan
Ganweriwala
Mohenjo Daro
Chanhu Daro
Dholavira
Lothal
SULAIMAN RANGE
BALUCHISTAN
CENTRAL MAKRAN RANGE
Jhelum
Ravi
Beas
Sutlej
Indus
Thar Desert
ARAVALI RANGE
ARABIAN SEA
0   250 miles
0   500 km

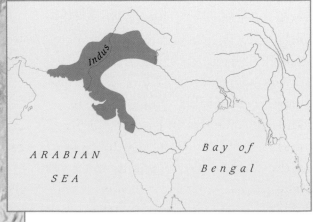
Indus
ARABIAN SEA
Bay of Bengal

INDUS VALLEY

3100–2600 BCE

First towns are built in the Indus valley.

2600–2000 BCE

The Indus civilization at its height included the great Indus cities Mohenjo Daro, Harappa, Ganweriwala, Rakhigari, and Dholavira.

2000–1700 BCE

Collapse of the Indus civilization.

Beginnings

In the middle of the fourth millennium BCE, the first farming people settled along the Indus valley. They lived in small villages in houses made of mud brick and raised wheat and barley. They also kept cattle, sheep, and goats.

Each summer the rivers flooded, swollen by snow melting and flowing down from the Himalayas. As the waters retreated in the autumn, the farmers planted their crops, which were ready for harvest the following spring. The land was so productive that the people were able to grow extra food, which could be traded or used to support specialist craftspeople. By 3100 BCE the first towns had appeared. With the towns came the beginning of the so-called Early Harappan period, which lasted for about 500 years.

Around 2600 BCE regional differences disappeared, and all the Indus people began to use the same type of pottery and live in the same way. This period saw the building of the world's first planned cities, at Harappa, Mohenjo Daro, Ganweriwala, Rakhigari, and Dholavira. The largest were Harappa and Mohenjo Daro, which may

INDUS VALLEY MUD BRICKS

The building bricks, both fired and of sun-dried mud, were all made to a standard size, with the ratios 1 (height) to 2 (width) to 4 (length).

▲ Harappa and the other Indus cities were very plain. There is no sign of any decoration on the brick walls.

have housed between 40,000 and 50,000 people. There were also hundreds of smaller Indus towns.

Cities

In other countries, villages grew into towns, which then grew into cities. In contrast, the Indus cities were planned as cities from the beginning. Where the ground was leveled for building, engineers laid out a neat north-south and east-west grid of streets.

Each city had a small "upper town" on its west side, which was built on a raised mud brick platform and surrounded by a wall. It may have been the center of government and perhaps also of religion. Most of the ordinary people lived and worked in the much larger lower town.

The cities had huge buildings believed to have been granaries. Used to store the wheat and barley grown in the countryside, these buildings provide further evidence of the Indus people's skill at planning and organization.

▲ This decorated pot and lid were found in a grave at Harappa. The fact that they buried the dead with goods suggests that Indus people believed in an afterlife.

Society

The varied sizes of the Indus houses suggest that there were different social classes with different levels of wealth. The Indus skill at organization and the lack of variation between sites has led some historians to believe that there was a strong central state and that the Indus people had a real empire, perhaps with a capital at Mohenjo Daro or Harappa. However, it is also possible that they simply liked doing things in a particular way wherever they lived and were able to organize life for themselves without powerful rulers.

Water Management

The greatest achievement of the Indus people was their water supply management. They collected rainwater and built dams on rivers to collect the water, which was then stored in huge reservoirs. Each city had its own reservoir, and each house had its own well or shared a communal well with a few other houses. Almost every Indus house had a toilet and bathing platform. Streets had gutters and well-built sewers to carry off waste from toilets. The Indus concern with personal cleanliness would not be matched again until Roman times, over two thousand years later.

Trade and Crafts

In the lower town of every Indus city, there were workshops where jewelry and luxury goods were made, including carnelian beads, pearl necklaces, and ornaments made from lapis lazuli, elephant ivory, gold, glazed pottery, and shells.

The Indus people used the rivers and the sea to trade their goods with people in distant lands. Indus products have been found as far away as the Arabian Gulf. Imported goods included gold and jade from southern India, silver and tin from Mesopotamia, copper and lapis lazuli from Afghanistan, and turquoise from Iran.

Writing

Despite many attempts to do so, the Indus script has not been deciphered. One problem is that nothing is known of the language that Indus people spoke. Another is that writing was used only for short inscriptions on pottery and seals. All that is known is that the script had over three hundred characters, mostly picture signs, such as a fish or a wheel, and that each one probably stood for a single syllable.

INDUS SEALS

Archaeologists have found many small seals, carved from a soft stone called steatite, as well as the clay impressions they made. These seals often have cord or sack marks on the back, suggesting that they were used by merchants to identify bundles of goods.

Each Indus seal was decorated with a picture of an animal in profile, such as a bull, an elephant, a rhinoceros, an antelope, or a tiger. Above the animal was a line of letters in the Indus script, possibly spelling the name of the merchant.

▼ These clay impressions made by Indus seals show (clockwise from left) a bull, a rhinoceros, a tiger, and an elephant, each with the mysterious Indus writing above.

▲ *A pottery lamp in the shape of a woman wearing necklaces and a headdress. Such objects provide good evidence of how the Indus people dressed.*

INDUS TOYS

Archaeologists digging in Indus cities have found many small terra-cotta objects that seem to be toys. They include models of animals, such as cattle with nodding heads, begging dogs, and monkeys, and also wheeled carts pulled by oxen, pieces from games, pottery mazes, and whistles.

Clothes

Some of the most interesting pottery objects found by archaeologists are human figurines, which reveal how the Indus people dressed and wore their hair. They wore few articles of clothing, apart from loincloths, but covered themselves with jewelry, including necklaces, bracelets, ornamental belts, and nose ornaments. Women are often shown wearing fan-shaped headdresses. Men wore beards but shaved their upper lip and gathered their hair into a bun at the back of their head.

What Happened to the Indus Civilization?

Indus culture came to an end between 2000 and 1700 BCE. The cause is still a mystery. It may have been a natural disaster, such as a change in the climate or the Indus River shifting its course away from the cities. Other theories include foreign invasions, plagues, or a breakdown in the farming system caused by overpopulation. A combination of more than one factor may well have been to blame.

Whatever the cause, by 1700 BCE the Indus cities had all been abandoned. The memory of the Indus way of life was lost for nearly four thousand years, as there is no mention of it in any of the ancient Indian chronicles. It was not until the 1920s that archaeologists discovered the ruins of the Indus cities and began to uncover India's first great lost civilization.

SEE ALSO
- China • Egypt • Mesopotamia
- Mohenjo Daro

Ishtar

Ishtar was a goddess of love and war in Mesopotamian religion. Ishtar, an Akkadian name, was the name she was known by to the Babylonians. However, the worship of Ishtar gradually merged with the worship of Inanna, a Sumerian goddess of love and possibly of fertility. Later myths about Ishtar and Inanna therefore refer to the same goddess.

Ishtar is a complex figure in Mesopotamian religion and myth, sometimes known as the daughter of the sky god, An, and sometimes as the daughter of Enki, the god of the earth. She is also seen as the daughter of the moon god, Nanna, and sister of the sun god, Utu.

Shulgi, a king of the Sumerian city of Ur, was referred to as Ishtar's lover as a way of emphasizing his importance. Another Sumerian city, Erech (present-day Warka), was a center for followers of Inanna/Ishtar, and her marriage was celebrated there in a city festival around 3500 BCE. A temple dedicated to Ishtar has been excavated at Erech. In the Assyrian city of Nineveh, there was an important temple of Ishtar that flourished after 2000 BCE until the city was finally destroyed in 612 BCE. In Akkadian myth Ishtar was an astral deity. She was linked to the planet Venus, and her symbol may have been a star with six, eight, or sixteen rays, sometimes shown inside a circle.

◄ This eighth-century-BCE ivory plaque, found in the Assyrian palace at Calah, may represent Ishtar. The nose has been restored.

A VISIT TO THE UNDERWORLD

In one myth that has been preserved in writing, Ishtar took a hazardous journey to the underworld. After a struggle for power in the world of the dead, Ishtar was defeated and the living world became infertile. The earth god, Enki, then had to use all his skill to bring Ishtar's body back from the underworld. Enki provided magic water that restored her to life but only on condition that she leave someone else in the world of the dead.

Ishtar discovered that the god Dumuzi, her lover and a fertility figure who is also associated with Inanna in Sumerian myth, had not mourned her. Ishtar then chose him to take her place. Dumuzi tried his best to escape, but he was eventually captured and taken to the underworld. Taking turns with his younger sister, Dumuzi had to spend the six summer months in the world of the dead so that Ishtar could stay in the world of the living and make the land fertile.

Powerful and ambitious, Ishtar was a popular figure in Mesopotamian religion and mythology. The tale of the hero Gilgamesh tells how he rejected Ishtar's love. In another story Ishtar journeyed to the city of Eridu and, in a drunken bet, won valuable symbols of power from her father, the earth god Enki. The ending of this story is unclear because the clay tablets on which it was written are not well preserved.

▶ In this impression made by an Assyrian cylinder seal made of soapstone, the woman on the right with a star above her, receiving homage from another woman, is Ishtar. As a goddess of war, she is armed with a variety of weapons.

SEE ALSO

- Akkadians
- Erech
- Gilgamesh Epic
- Shulgi

Japan

Japan, a chain of islands in the Pacific Ocean off eastern Asia, was colonized by settlers from the Asian mainland in prehistoric times. Between 10,000 BCE and 500 CE Japan was influenced by the neighboring civilizations of China and Korea. It also developed a distinctive way of life and culture. Little is known about Japan's early history because writing did not develop there until the 400s CE.

Early History

Japan is made up of four large islands and thousands of smaller ones. In ancient times civilization developed first on the largest island, Honshu. Around 30,000 years ago settlers from Siberia and Korea arrived in Honshu. They came on foot over a natural bridge of land. Later, around 20,000 years ago, the sea level rose, and Japan was cut off from the Asian mainland.

Around 10,000 years ago a civilization, now called the Jomon culture, developed on Honshu's coastal plains. At first, the Jomon lived as nomads, hunting deer and pigs in the forests and gathering shellfish on the seashore. Later, around 3000 BCE, the Jomon moved inland and became more settled and began growing vegetables in gardens, making pottery, and using stone tools.

Civilization Develops

Around 2000 BCE the Jomon moved back to the coasts, where they learned to make boats and to fish. After 300 BCE more settlers reached Japan from China and Korea on the mainland. They brought new skills such as weaving, rice growing, mining, and metalworking. Soon Japanese smiths were making bronze and iron weapons and tools.

Between 300 BCE and 300 CE, a time known as the Yayoi period, the first villages developed. Gradually they grew larger and became the centers of small kingdoms. By

300 CE Honshu and the neighboring island of Kyushu were a patchwork of small kingdoms, each ruled by a powerful clan (a group of related families). Gradually one clan from western Honshu, called the Yamato, became more powerful than all the others and through war and alliances slowly took over the whole country. Around 500 CE the Yamato became emperors of a united Japan.

▼ The formation of states in early Japan, 300 BCE to 300 CE.

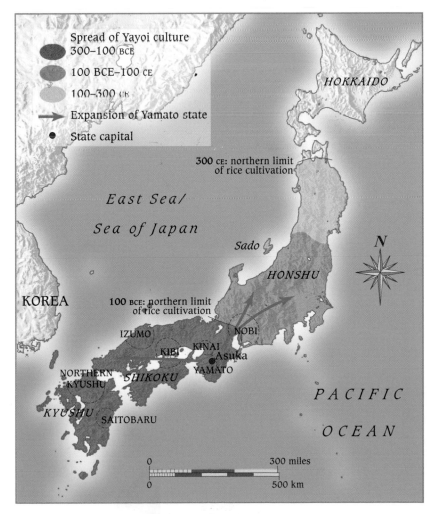

Spread of Yayoi culture
- 300–100 BCE
- 100 BCE–100 CE
- 100–300 CE
- → Expansion of Yamato state
- • State capital

300 CE: northern limit of rice cultivation

East Sea/ Sea of Japan

HOKKAIDO

Sado

HONSHU

N

100 BCE: northern limit of rice cultivation

KOREA

IZUMO

NOBI

KIBI

KINAI

Asuka

YAMATO

NORTHERN KYUSHU

SHIKOKU

KYUSHU

SAITOBARU

PACIFIC OCEAN

0   300 miles
0   500 km

JAPAN

30,000 BCE
Japan is first settled.

10,000–300 BCE
The Jomon period.

300 BCE–300 CE
The Yayoi period.

300–700 CE
The Kofun period.

▼ This nineteenth-century Japanese print shows farmers engaged in the physically demanding work of planting rice seedlings in flooded paddy fields.

The time between 300 and 700 CE is known as the Kofun period, named after the large earth burial mounds, called *kofun*, in which the clans buried their chiefs. Tall clay statues of warriors and servants, called haniwa, were placed around the tombs to guard them.

Meanwhile the neighboring civilizations of China and Korea continued to influence Japan. In the 400s the Chinese philosophy Confucianism spread to Japan, around the same time that the Japanese began to use the Chinese method of writing. During the 500s the Buddhist religion was brought to Japan by Chinese and Korean monks.

Emperors of Japan

Japanese emperors of the Yamato clan, claiming they were descended from the sun goddess, Amaterasu, were honored as gods themselves, and people bowed low whenever they appeared. The emperor acted as high priest, asking Amaterasu for favors on behalf of ordinary people. He was commander in chief of the army, the highest judge, and the main lawgiver all rolled into one.

Food and Farming

Farming developed in Japan around 3000 BCE. After 300 BCE the main crop was rice. On flat land and terraced hillsides rice was grown in flooded paddy fields, or *tanbo*. Fish were also reared in the paddies. Farmers grew wheat, barley, red beans, soybeans, fruits, and vegetables. Most peasants did not own their own land. Instead

RELIGION IN ANCIENT JAPAN

The ancient religion of Japan is called Shinto, a word meaning "the way of the gods." Shintoism began in Japan during the Jomon period and is still practiced. The highest Shinto deity is Amaterasu, the sun goddess. Amaterasu was originally worshiped only by the Yamato, but after 500 CE she was honored throughout Japan. People also worshiped other gods called kami. They were the spirits of natural features, such as rivers and mountains, or the ghosts of important people who had died.

they worked fields owned by wealthy noblemen and paid a portion of each harvest to the lord in rent.

Arts and Crafts

Since ancient times the Japanese have been skilled craft workers. The Jomon were among the first civilizations in the world to make pottery. By about 3000 BCE they were decorating pots and vases with beautiful patterns and had learned to fire clay. The ancient Japanese were also skilled smiths and carvers of stone and wood. During the Jomon period artisans learned to make lacquerware by painting wooden bowls with a special tree sap called lacquer. The liquid sap dries to form a hard, glossy surface. Lacquerware is still made all over Japan.

◀ A haniwa (clay statue) of a warrior from the sixth century CE. The people of Japan probably believed that these statues would serve great lords in the life after death.

SEE ALSO
- Amaterasu
- Buddhism • China
- Chinese Philosophy
- Confucianism
- Farming • Pottery
- Religion

Jericho

Jericho, situated in what is now the West Bank area of Palestine, is possibly the oldest town in the world. About ten thousand years ago the first farmers started growing crops in western Asia. At that time people gradually changed from pursuing a nomadic hunter-gatherer existence and began to form settled communities. Jericho was one of these ancient community settlements.

A Walled Town

The region around Jericho is now very dry but was less so in ancient times. The town probably grew up on this particular site because it had a permanent spring. The water from the spring made the surrounding land muddy and damp, the perfect conditions for cereal farming. The crops grew well, and by 7000 BCE the town had grown to about 2.4 acres (1.6 hectares). To protect their spring and their prosperous settlement, the people built a town wall ten feet (3 m) thick. The wall was strengthened on the western side by a thirty-foot (9 m) high tower, which had an internal passageway and a trapdoor entrance. Jericho thus became one of the earliest defended sites. Over the next five thousand years, through the biblical period, it was several times destroyed, abandoned, and rebuilt.

Farming and Hunting

Archaeological evidence shows that the most widely grown crops in Jericho were wheat and barley. Between 8000 and 7000 BCE the people were still hunting, and the gazelle was the main source of meat. Sometime between 7000 and 6000 BCE the gazelle was replaced by domesticated sheep and goats (which provided 40 percent of the people's meat intake), along with cattle, pigs, and horses. Gazelles, deer, and foxes, however, were still hunted and still accounted for 32 percent of the diet of Jericho's residents.

Did the Walls Come Tumbling Down?

In a famous incident in the Old Testament, Joshua's army shook the walls of Jericho to the ground by parading and blowing trumpets outside the city. Archaeologists, however, have never found any evidence in support of this claim. The collapsed walls that were found in the 1930s dated from between 3000 and 2000 BCE. As Joshua lived in about 1150 BCE, the two events could not be connected. Kathleen Kenyon,

▼ *This skull of a young woman, found at Jericho, dates from the seventh millennium BCE. Her features were modeled in plaster, and cowrie shells were used to represent her eyes.*

ONE FASCINATING FIND WAS A GROUP OF PLASTER SKULLS, MODELED TO LOOK LIKE THEIR OWNERS. THE SKULLS MAY BE EVIDENCE OF ANCESTOR WORSHIP:

It took five days to extract them all and it was a triumph of patient work. . . . But the family group of seven heads was well worth our trouble. They were all most remarkable as realistic human portraits. . . . The features, nose, mouth, ears and eyebrows are molded with extraordinary delicacy. . . . I have personally always been convinced that they are the heads of venerated ancestors, largely owing to the loving care which the skilful modelling of the features suggests.

KATHLEEN KENYON, *EXCAVATIONS AT JERICHO*

an archaeologist who excavated the town in the 1950s, found that Jericho was not even inhabited during Joshua's time and was rebuilt only in the seventh century BCE. It seems that the damage done to the early walls may have been caused by an earthquake.

Working at Jericho between 1952 and 1956, Kenyon provided soil samples containing ancient pollen and grain seeds for William Libby, the chemist who developed the carbon dating process at the University of Chicago. Other archaeologists were amazed when the samples were dated to the eighth and seventh millennia BCE. This evidence proved that agriculture had actually started over two thousand years earlier than had previously been thought.

This sixteenth-century painting by Raphael shows Joshua's army and the fall of Jericho. Excavations have shown, however, that the collapsed walls predated Joshua by over a thousand years and were probably caused by an earthquake.

SEE ALSO
• Farming • Judaism

Jerusalem

Jerusalem, an ancient city in present-day Israel, has been fought over many times and has seen many different rulers in its long history. The city was founded sometime in the third millennium BCE, probably by a Canaanite tribe who worshiped a god called Salem. (Jerusalem means "foundation of the god Salem.") Built on a hill with valleys on three of its sides, their settlement made it a good natural stronghold. It had its own water supply, vital in this hot dry country, and it was also situated alongside an ancient trade route, a pass through the hills.

▼ The Dome of the Rock, a beautiful seventh-century-CE Muslim mosque, now stands where the ancient Jewish temple once stood.

King David's City

Around 1000 BCE Jerusalem, then belonging to a people called the Jebusites, was conquered by King David, who had united the Hebrew tribes of Israel and Judah under his leadership. He made the city his royal capital and brought with him the Ark of the Covenant.

After David's death, around 965 BCE, his son and successor, Solomon, built a temple for the ark at the highest point of the city on a hill called Zion. From this time on, the city itself would also often be called Zion, or Mount Zion.

Solomon's Temple

According to the Bible, Solomon's temple was a rectangular stone building with two bronze pillars at the front and a flat wooden roof. It was richly decorated inside with cedar panels inlaid with gold. There was a large chamber and a small inner sanctuary, the Holy of Holies, where the ark was placed. In a courtyard in front of the temple, there was an altar for sacrifice and a great bronze basin, called the molten sea, for ritual washing.

Capital of Judah

When Solomon died in 928 BCE, the northern tribes split away and formed their

own kingdom of Israel. Jerusalem remained the capital of the southern kingdom, Judah, which was ruled by around twenty kings between 928 and 587 BCE.

Eventually, in 587 or 586 BCE, the city was captured by King Nebuchadrezzar of Babylon after an eighteen-month siege. The whole city was burned to the ground, and the surviving Jews were sent away to Babylon.

Almost fifty years later King Cyrus of Persia conquered Babylon and allowed the Jews to return to Jerusalem. The returning exiles rebuilt the walls of Jerusalem and the temple on a modest scale.

Hellenistic City

After Alexander the Great conquered the Persian Empire (333–331 BCE), the city came under the rule of Hellenistic (Greek) kings. Many of the leading Jews began to speak Greek and dress in Greek clothes. In 167 BCE King Antiochus of Syria tried to rededicate the Jewish temple to the Greek god Zeus. This act set off a successful Jewish revolt. The rebel leaders, the Maccabees, rededicated the temple to God. For the next century, the Maccabean family ruled the Jewish state.

▲ An artist's impression of the vast temple built by Herod the Great between 20 and 18 BCE.

THE ARK OF THE COVENANT

The Ark of the Covenant was an ancient Hebrew box, made of wood and covered with gold. It was built to hold the stone tablets on which were written the Ten Commandments given by God to Moses. The ark was seen as a sign that God had entered into a covenant, or agreement, with the Hebrews. He would protect and favor them if they worshiped him and obeyed his laws. God himself was thought to be present in the ark.

▶ After destroying the Jewish temple, the Romans carried its treasures through Rome in a triumphal procession (a victory parade), a scene shown on this arch built by the emperor Titus.

Roman Rule

The Romans conquered western Asia in 64 and 63 BCE. In the Jewish homeland they set up a king wholly under Roman influence, Herod the Great, who reigned from 37 to 4 BCE. Although Herod spent much of his time at Caesarea, Jerusalem remained the most important place on earth for Jews, who gathered there every year for great festivals. To win popularity, Herod rebuilt the temple on a grand scale.

Jerusalem's Jewish history came to a violent end after two unsuccessful uprisings against Roman rule, 66 to 73 CE and 132 to 136. The temple was destroyed, and Jews were forbidden to enter the city.

Christianity

In the fourth century CE Jerusalem took on a new importance when Emperor Constantine made Christianity the official religion of the Roman Empire. His mother, Helena, traveled to the city to find the sites linked with the life of Jesus Christ, who had died there. Soon the city was filled with churches.

Jerusalem was captured by Arabs in 638 CE and became an equally holy city to Muslims. Jerusalem remains a holy city for three world religions: Judaism, Christianity, and Islam.

MANY OF THE PSALMS (JEWISH HYMNS AND LAMENTS) IN THE OLD TESTAMENT DESCRIBE THE BEAUTY OF JERUSALEM AND ITS IMPORTANCE AS A HOLY CITY:

Great is the Lord, and greatly to be praised in the city of our God, in the mountain of his holiness. Beautiful for situation, the joy of the whole earth, is Mount Zion, on the sides of the north, the city of the great king.

PSALM 48: 1–2 (KJV)

SEE ALSO

- Alexander the Great • Babylonians
- Christianity • Constantine • David
- Dead Sea Scrolls • Hebrews
- Jesus of Nazareth • Judaism • Masada
- Moses • Nebuchadrezzar II

Jesus of Nazareth

The life and teachings of Jesus (c. 6 BCE–c. 29 CE) are at the center of Christianity. Jesus lived in Nazareth, near the Sea of Galilee, in present-day Israel. As a young man he began to preach and soon gathered a group of followers. The Roman and Jewish authorities feared his influence, and when he was only in his early thirties, he was executed as a political and religious rebel. Christians worship him as the Son of God, and his message guides their lives and behavior.

The Gospels

Jesus did not leave any writings behind. The story of his life is told in the first four books of the New Testament, Matthew, Mark, Luke, and John, known as the Gospels (*gospel* means "God's word"). Written between forty and seventy years after Jesus' death, the Gospels were the basis of religious teaching in early Christian churches. They often blend factual accounts with descriptions of miraculous events. In a number of ways, the accounts are different from each other. Thus the evidence the Gospels provide about the actual life of Jesus is not entirely harmonious. The Christian versions of events are virtually the only complete ones that survive. Some historians claim that a critical view of Jesus' life is thus impossible to attain.

Early Life

According to the New Testament, Jesus was born in Bethlehem. His mother, Mary, and his father, a carpenter named Joseph, had traveled a long way from their home in Nazareth to be registered as taxpayers by the Romans. The inns were full, so Mary had to give birth in a stable. The Gospels contain very little information about Jesus' life as a boy or a teenager.

▶ *One of the most famous stories from Jesus's life, his birth, or Nativity, is depicted in this eleventh-century mosaic from a monastery in Greece. Mary was said to have given birth in a stable.*

Baptism

Just before he was thirty, according to the Gospels, Jesus met a preacher named John the Baptist, who lived in the desert. John the Baptist believed that history would end very soon and that God would judge everyone in the world. In preparation for this Last Judgment, he baptized people (washed them with water as a sign of repentance of sin), including Jesus.

Being baptized was a turning point in Jesus' life. According to the New Testament, a voice came out of the clouds, announcing that Jesus was the Son of God. Jesus then spent forty days and forty nights alone in the desert, where he contemplated his future. He returned to Galilee and began preaching.

Jesus the Preacher

Jesus traveled around preaching, in the manner of a teacher, through stories called parables, which everyone could understand. His message was that God was just but also loving and merciful toward everyone, regardless of background or gender. In return, God expected all people to love one another. Moreover, as God was about to bring his kingdom of heaven to earth, it was important to obey Jesus' call to follow him. Jesus chose twelve disciples (the Twelve Apostles), including a tax collector, a fisherman, and a farmer, and instructed them to spread his message.

Holy Week

The last week of Jesus' life is recounted in all four Gospels. On Sunday Jesus went to Jerusalem, where he was welcomed by a huge crowd, who hailed him as the Messiah, the king who the Jews believed would restore the old Jewish kingdom of Israel. On Monday, Tuesday, and Wednesday, Jesus debated, preached, and predicted his own death. On Thursday he ate his last meal, known as the Last Supper, with his disciples.

Jesus the Rebel

It was very dangerous for Jesus in Jerusalem. The Romans said Jesus was a political rebel. The Jews said he was a blasphemer. After the Last Supper, Judas Iscariot, one of the Twelve, told Roman soldiers that Jesus had gone to the Garden of Gethsemane, outside Jerusalem, to pray. They arrested Jesus there and handed him to the Jewish authorities, who passed him

▼ *This sixteenth-century painting by Francesco Bacchiacca shows the baptism of Jesus by John.*

to the Roman governor, Pontius Pilate. Pilate sentenced Jesus to death. On Friday morning Jesus was crucified, an especially slow and painful way to die.

Resurrection

According to the Gospels, Jesus was taken down from the cross late on Friday and placed in a tomb. On Sunday a woman named Mary Magdalene went to the tomb to prepare Jesus for burial, but his body was not there. Angels announced that Jesus was alive. Jesus then appeared to his disciples for a period of forty days, before ascending into heaven.

Conclusion

These miraculous events proved to Jesus' followers that he was the Messiah of Jewish tradition. In Greek he was called the Christ, meaning "the one anointed as king" (an incarnation of God himself). These events were the starting point for Christianity.

THIS PASSAGE DESCRIBES JESUS AND HIS APOSTLES AT THE LAST SUPPER. CHRISTIANS ALL OVER THE WORLD REPEAT THIS CEREMONY, DRINKING WINE AND EATING BREAD IN MEMORY OF JESUS' DEATH:

And he took bread, and brake it, and gave unto them, saying, "This is my body which is given for you: this do in remembrance of me." Likewise also the cup after supper, saying, "This cup is the new testament in my blood, which is shed for you."

LUKE 22:19–20 (KJV)

▲ *This third-century relief of the Last Supper was carved on a sarcophagus (stone coffin) found near Rome.*

SEE ALSO

- Christianity • Jerusalem • Judaism
- Paul of Tarsus • Religion

Jewelry

Jewelry is any object worn as personal adornment, such as necklaces, beads, crowns, hairpins, earrings, and bracelets. Some of the world's oldest jewelry was made twenty-five thousand years ago by the Stone Age hunters of Europe and Asia, who strung animal teeth and shells into necklaces and carved pieces of bone and ivory from the tusks of mammoths into bracelets.

▼ Jewelry made from gold and semiprecious stones, as would be worn by a female member of the royal court in the Sumerian city of Ur, around 2550 BCE.

The Function of Jewelry

The main function of jewelry was to beautify the wearer. However, jewelry was also a sign of wealth. By wearing it, people were literally putting their riches on display. Jewelry was also worn to demonstrate a person's position in society—kings and queens wore crowns; commoners did not. It was also believed that jewelry had magical properties and could protect the wearer from harm. In ancient Egypt the jewelry worn by men, women, and children was valued as much for its protective qualities as for its decorative effect.

On a practical level jewelry could be used to keep hairstyles neat and fasten clothes.

Sumerian Jewelry

One famous discovery of ancient jewelry was made in the 1920s by the English archaeologist Leonard Woolley (1880–1960) in the Sumerian city of Ur in present-day southern Iraq. Woolley and his team excavated a cemetery dating to around 2500 BCE. The nobles of Ur had been buried there with large quantities of jewelry made from gold, silver, exotic shells, and rare stones such as lapis lazuli (dark blue), chalcedony (white), and carnelian (red and orange). The men wore gold headbands with large beads at the front and a gold chain at the back. Women wore headdresses of golden flowers and leaves, crescent-shaped earrings, chokers around their necks, pins to fasten their clothes, and cloaks made of beads.

A first-century-CE Roman cameo carved from onyx, a fine-grained semiprecious stone that has bands of color within it. Here the white band has been carved into scenes that stand out against the darker background band.

Roman Jewelry

Roman women, especially from the upper classes, wore many items of jewelry. All women wore a fibula, a brooch that held the wearer's clothes in place. An expensive fibula might be made of gold and highly decorated, while a cheaper one would be made of plain bronze. Hairpins were used to secure a woman's hair. Gold coins were set into pendants, armbands, body chains, and belts, all of which were articles of female adornment.

Finger rings were worn by men and women. It was the custom for Roman men to wear a signet ring set with an engraved gemstone (an intaglio). This signet ring was used to make an impression in sealing wax in order to seal and authorize documents.

It was the custom at first to wear rings on a single finger only, the one next to the little finger, and this we see to be the case in the statues of Numa and Servius Tullius. Later it became usual to put rings on the finger next to the thumb, even with statues of the gods; and more recently still it has been the fashion to wear them upon the little finger too. Among the Gauls and Britons the middle finger, it is said, is used for the purpose. At the present day, however, with us, this is the only finger that is excepted, for all the others are loaded with rings, smaller rings even being separately adapted for the smaller joints of the fingers.

PLINY THE ELDER (C. 23–79 CE), NATURAL HISTORY, BOOK 33

Cameos were precious or semiprecious stones with designs carved in relief, giving them a three-dimensional quality. A cameo was an ornamental item, set into rings, pendants, and brooches. Children wore an amulet known as a *bulla*—a lucky charm.

Chinese Jewelry

In ancient China, jade was prized for its spiritual and magical properties. From about 1000 BCE jewelers carved jade into amulets in the shape of buffalo, fish, birds, and stags. In later times jade carvers produced increasingly ornate items, decorated with designs of birds, dragons, and human figures.

All Chinese women wore hairpins. At first made from bone or jade, hairpins were later made from gold. Belt plaques were the main jewelry item worn by men. These small squares were made from jade or agate (another type of hard stone) and were fixed to the man's leather or silk belt. Some belt plaques were carved with figures or landscapes.

SEE ALSO
- China
- Roman Republic and Empire
- Ur

▲ *A third-century-BCE Chinese ornament made from carved jade, worn by a man on his waist belt.*

GRANULATION: THE LOST ART OF SUMERIAN JEWELERS

Sumerian jewelers discovered the technique of granulation, in which granules (grains) of gold could be fixed to a piece of jewelry. The granules were probably made by melting gold and dripping it into cold water. As the drips sank, they split into perfect tiny spheres. Great skill was needed to solder (join) the miniature balls to the jewelry — a technique that was rediscovered only in 1933. The jewelry was coated with a paste of glue and copper oxide, and the granules were pressed into it. The object was heated and the copper oxide formed a solder to which the grains of gold stuck.

Josephus, Flavius

A Jewish historian and soldier, Flavius Josephus (37–c. 100 CE) is the main source of information on the Jewish War and the early history of the Jewish people.

▼ A Roman bust of the Jewish historian Flavius Josephus.

Life in Judaea

Flavius Josephus was born into a family of priests in Jerusalem as Yosef ben Mattityahu, a Hebrew name meaning Joseph, son of Matthias. He did so well in his studies, he later said, that, by the age of fourteen, Jewish scholars were consulting him. At sixteen he studied the teachings of three Jewish sects (the Sadducees, Essenes, and Pharisees). Unable to decide which sect to follow, he then spent three years in the wilderness of Judaea, living as a hermit. When he returned to Jerusalem, he chose to become a Pharisee.

In 64 CE, aged twenty-six, he went to Rome to ask Emperor Nero to release some Jewish priests who had been sent there for trial. It was a successful mission, but on his return ben Mattiyahu found the Roman-ruled province of Judaea about to rebel against the Roman Empire.

The Jewish War (66–73 CE)

At first, ben Mattityahu was opposed to the Jewish rebellion. In 66 CE he became a general whose duty was to defend Galilee, a district in the northern part of Judaea. However, a year later, when Roman forces captured the fortress of Jotapata, ben Mattiyahu escaped with some companions. Rather than be hunted down, they all agreed to end their own lives. When all but one of his companions had committed suicide, ben Mattiyahu gave himself up to the Roman general Vespasian.

A Change of Name

While a prisoner of the Romans, ben Mattityahu predicted that Vespasian would become the next Roman emperor. When this prediction came true (Vespasian became emperor in 69 CE), Vespasian granted ben Mattityahu his freedom, made him a Roman citizen, and gave him a house in Rome, a pension, and land in Judaea. Vespasian also adopted ben Mattityahu as a member of his own family. The Jewish soldier took the emperor's family name, Flavius, and became known by the Roman name of Flavius Josephus.

Josephus the Historian

Josephus spent the rest of his life in Rome, where he devoted himself to writing. Between about 75 and 79 he published *The Jewish War*, a seven-volume account of the failed Jewish rebellion, and in about 94 he published *The Jewish Antiquities*, a twenty-volume history of the Jews. The works of Flavius Josephus are important because they provide historical background for the Jewish faith and for the beginnings of Christianity. Josephus was writing at the same time that Christian authors were composing some of the books of the New Testament.

▶ *A page from a fifteenth-century French version of Josephus's book on the Jewish War. The illustration shows a town under siege and Josephus surrendering to the Roman emperor.*

SEE ALSO

• Jesus of Nazareth • Judaism • Masada
• Nero • Roman Republic and Empire

THIS IS THE ONLY FIRST-CENTURY-CE TEXT BY A NON-CHRISTIAN WRITER TO MENTION JESUS CHRIST:

At this time there appeared Jesus, a wise man, if indeed one should call him a man. For he was a doer of startling deeds, a teacher of the people who receive the truth with pleasure. And he gained a following both among many Jews and among many of Greek origin. He was the Messiah.

FLAVIUS JOSEPHUS, *THE JEWISH ANTIQUITIES*, BOOK 18

Judaism

Judaism is the religion of the Jews, a people also known as Hebrews and Israelites. Judaism was the first successful religion based on monotheism, the belief in a single god.

The Jews saw their god, whose personal name is Yahweh, as the creator of everything. He was all-powerful and universal (everywhere). Yet he was also a personal god, directly concerned with the behavior of every individual. This belief in a single universal yet personal god later led to two new religions, Christianity and Islam.

A Holy Nation

Jews believe that Yahweh chose them as a special holy nation. In order to live in a holy way, Jews had to obey a mass of religious laws. The most important was the requirement to worship no other gods. Jews also had to set aside one day of the week, the Sabbath, for rest. They were forbidden to eat certain animal foods, such as pork and shellfish, which were called unclean. Animals permitted for food had to be killed and cooked in a particular way. The aim of these laws was to build a just society on earth in accordance with Yahweh's wishes.

Although gentiles (non-Jews) can convert to Judaism, most Jews are born into the religion. Judaism regards Jews as God's chosen people, and all those who are Jewish by birth are believed to be descended on the maternal side from their ancestor Abraham. Boys are circumcised as a mark of their membership in the Jewish race.

Festivals and Fasts

The Jewish year includes several great festivals, marking the changing seasons as well as important events in Jewish history. Passover was an ancient spring festival that became linked with the story of the Jews' escape from Egypt.

According to the story, the Jews had been made slaves of the Egyptian pharaoh but were rescued when God sent a series of plagues (disasters) to punish the Egyptians. The worst plague was the killing of all the Egyptian firstborn children by an angel, who "passed over" the homes of the Jews but struck the homes of the Egyptians. The Jews were believed to have left Egypt in such a hurry that they had no time to add yeast to make their bread rise. In memory of this deliverance, during Passover, Jews eat only flat bread without yeast.

As well as the festivals, there are a number of special times when Jews fast, or give up food, drink, and other pleasures. The most important fast day is Yom Kippur, when people fast for an entire day to atone to Yahweh for their sinfulness during the previous year.

▼ Jews believe that God miraculously parted the Red Sea to allow them to escape from Egypt, a scene shown in this 1634 French painting.

Worshiping Yahweh

Judaism changed over time. In the second millennium BCE, when the Jews lived in separate tribes, Yahweh was worshiped at sanctuaries (holy places), often on hilltops. He was offered sacrifices—animals, such as lambs and goats, that were killed and burned on raised stone platforms called altars.

According to the Bible, around 1000 BCE King David, who had united the tribes, conquered Jerusalem, which became the capital of a Jewish kingdom. David's son Solomon built a temple in Jerusalem. The Jerusalem temple became the most important place to worship Yahweh. Even so, Jews continued to offer sacrifices in other temples and sanctuaries.

▶ *Since Christianity is an offshoot of Judaism, stories of ancient Jewish history have always been important to Christians. This medieval painting shows the conquest of Jerusalem by the Babylonians in the sixth century BCE.*

WHY JUST ONE GOD?

There are different ideas about why the Jews, unlike all other ancient peoples, chose to worship just one god. The Jews' own version, in the Hebrew Bible, is that Yahweh revealed himself as the one true god to a series of teachers and leaders. The greatest of these was Moses, a man who may have lived in the thirteenth century BCE. The Bible says that Yahweh gave Moses a set of laws, the most important of which forbade worship of other gods. However, as the stories of Moses were written down hundreds of years after his lifetime by Jews who strongly believed in just one god, their portrayal of Moses may have been influenced by their own beliefs.

▼ Moses is depicted holding up God's laws, in this seventeenth-century French painting.

Monotheism (the belief in just one god) may have developed gradually. It was preached from the tenth to the sixth centuries BCE by a succession of prophets—men and women believed to speak on behalf of Yahweh. Despite these prophets, many Jews continued to worship other gods alongside Yahweh until the sixth century BCE.

An artist's reconstruction of ruins at Qumran, by the Dead Sea, which may have been home to members of a Jewish sect called the Essenes.

Disaster

In 587 or 586 BCE the Jews suffered a great disaster: they were conquered by the Babylonians. The holy temple was destroyed, and the Jews were taken away to live in Babylon.

The time they spent in Babylon changed Judaism in a number of ways. Jews began to look back at their history in order to learn why Yahweh had abandoned them. The answer seemed to be that they had been punished for failing to obey his laws. After the exile Judaism became a much stricter religion. No Jew would now worship other gods.

Around 538 BCE the Jews were allowed to return home and rebuild their temple. The Jerusalem temple was now the only place where sacrifices could be offered, and the temple priests became much more important.

In these years, the Hebrew Bible began to take shape. For Jews, the most important books of the Bible are the first five, called the Torah ("instruction") in Hebrew and the Pentateuch ("five books") in Greek. As well as recording Jewish history from the creation of the world onwards, the Torah contains hundreds of laws covering Jewish worship and everyday life.

DURING THE SECOND TEMPLE PERIOD THE VARIOUS JEWISH SECTS HAD DIFFERENT IDEAS ABOUT DEATH:

The Essenes declare that for the good souls there waits a home beyond the ocean, troubled by neither rain nor snow nor heat but refreshed by a wind that blows gently from the ocean. They send bad souls to a dark, stormy pit, full of endless punishments. . . . For the Pharisees, every soul is immortal, but only the souls of good men pass into other bodies, while the souls of bad men suffer eternal punishment. . . . The Sadducees utterly deny the permanence of the soul, punishments, and rewards.

JOSEPHUS, THE JEWISH WAR (LATE FIRST CENTURY CE)

The Second Temple

The time after the return from Babylon is known as the Second Temple period. These were troubled years for the Jews, who were ruled by one foreign power after another. Many Jews began to hope for a messiah, a man sent by Yahweh to restore their lost kingdom and bring peace and justice to the earth.

Judaism split into different sects, or groups. The temple priests were now called the Sadducees (after Zadok, the high priest under Solomon). They were opposed by the Pharisees, scholars who studied the Torah and applied it to everyday life. The Essenes believed that the only way to live a holy life was to retreat from the world.

Destruction of the Temple

In 66 CE the Jewish people rose up against Roman rule. This uprising was another disaster for Judaism. In 70 CE it led to the total destruction of the Jerusalem temple. All that remains of the temple is the western wall of its platform. This site is still the holiest place in the world for Jews.

Synagogues and Rabbis

The destruction of the temple and the spread of Jews to other lands led to the need for a new place of worship. The synagogue, a Greek word meaning "assembly," became the new center where Jews would meet to read their holy books.

Since there was now no temple sacrifice, there was no need for priests. The place of the priest was taken by a rabbi ("master" or "teacher"). Rabbis studied the Torah and wrote commentaries on it, working out how it could be applied to every imaginable situation. The earliest commentaries were collected in a book called the Mishnah. The Mishnah was then put together with later commentaries on the Mishnah to make a book called the Talmud.

Around the beginning of the first millennium, a well-known rabbi named Hillel was asked by a non-Jew, "Teach me the whole of the Law while I am standing on one leg." Hillel replied, "What is hateful to you, do not do to others. This is all the Law; the rest is commentary. Now go and study."

With rabbis, the synagogue, the Mishnah, and the Talmud, Judaism had taken on the form that it still has.

▼ *A page from a sixteenth-century copy of the Talmud.*

Kakadu Region

In northern Australia, around 150 miles (250 km) from the modern city of Darwin, lies Kakadu, a region that has been inhabited by aboriginal people for probably more than 50,000 years. The ancient people who lived there left many paintings in caves and on rocks and stones. There are no written records of aboriginal history, but scholars have learned a great deal from these cave paintings and from aboriginal legends of dreamtime (a time long ago when the earth was first created).

Continuous Settlement

Kakadu gets its name from the aboriginal word Gagadju, the name of one of the local aboriginal languages. Modern-day Gagadju-speaking aboriginals and other aboriginal groups are probably descended from the area's original settlers of over 50,000 years ago. The ancestors of the first arrivals to Kakadu may have come from Southeast Asia. For almost the whole of the last 50,000 years, these people have sheltered in caves or on the plains in simple but effective shelters covered in tree bark.

Living Off the Land

Kakadu has fifty species of mammals, two hundred types of birds, and over a thousand different plants in its eight thousand square miles (2,072,000 hectares). Many of these different plants and creatures provided the ancient people with a varied diet. Over generations, aboriginals learned which creatures should be avoided, such as venomous snakes, and which were easy to hunt and good to eat.

Six Seasons

Because the weather has always varied greatly in Kakadu, aboriginals divide the year into six seasons: Gujewg (January and February), Banggereng (March), Yegge (April and May), Wurrgeng (June and July), Gurrung (August and September), and Gunumeleng (October to December).

In each season these ancient people lived and ate in different ways. For example, in Yegge aboriginals burned small patches of land to encourage new plant growth. In Gurrung they hunted snakes and long-necked turtles in the water.

Rock Art

There are about five thousand rock art sites in the Kakadu region. The rock paintings show many animals, hunting scenes, and mythical creatures or spirits connected to

▼ *Prior to the rainy season, known as Gujewg, aboriginals often sought shelter on higher ground. The Anbangbang shelter at Nourlangie Rock, shown here, has been used for around 20,000 years.*

3500 **3000** **2500** **2000** **1500** **1000** **500** **1** **500**

KAKADU REGION

Before 50,000 BCE

Aboriginals reached and settled in the Kakadu region.

c. 50,000–6000 BCE

First period of rock art in Kakadu, known as pre-estuarine, mainly shows stick figures drawn in red ochers.

6000 BCE–c. 500 CE

Second period of rock art in Kakadu, called estuarine, mainly shows images of creatures that live in estuaries (waters where rivers meet the sea), such as barramundi fish and saltwater crocodiles.

2000 BCE

X-ray style of painting, showing the bones and insides of creatures, started in Kakadu.

c. 500 CE

The third period of rock art is called the freshwater period, as some of the lands of northern Kakadu became freshwater swamps.

THE LIGHTNING MAN
AND THE RAINBOW SERPENT

Two of the most important figures in aboriginal mythology are found in paintings in Kakadu. Ngalyod, also known as Almudj, the Rainbow Serpent, is believed to have created water holes as well as bringing the rainy season every year. Namarrgon, also known as Namarrkun, the Lightning Man, is believed to cause thunder by striking clouds with stone axes attached to his elbows and knees.

aboriginal dreamtime beliefs. Many were painted using ground-up rocks called ochers. The ochers were sometimes mixed with blood or berry juice to produce strong colors.

SEE ALSO
• Aboriginal Culture
• Art • Uluru

▶ This richly colored aboriginal artwork shows the rainbow serpent and witchetty grubs.

Kalidasa

Kalidasa, who may have lived around 400 CE, is widely thought to be the greatest Indian writer. A poet who wrote in Sanskrit, Kalidasa has been likened to the famous English playwright William Shakespeare and nicknamed the Sanskrit Shakespeare.

Almost nothing is known of Kalidasa's life. It is not even known when he lived, though he is generally thought to have been employed as a court writer by King Chandra Gupta II, who reigned from about 380 to 415 CE.

▼ A nineteenth-century wood engraving of a scene from the play Sakuntala by Kalidasa.

Kalidasa means "servant of Kali," the fierce Indian mother goddess. According to one legend, the poet was so devoted to this goddess that she rewarded him by giving him the gift of wisdom. This story is just one of many told about Kalidasa after his death. They say less about the poet himself than about his growing fame as a writer.

Judging by his writings, Kalidasa was a great traveler. He gives detailed descriptions of many different Indian landscapes, animals, and plants. Such travel was made possible by the peace and good order of the Gupta Empire which lasted from around 320 to 570 CE.

Plays and Poems

Kalidasa wrote three plays to be performed at court. Each of them deals with a king who falls in love. The most famous is *Abhijnana-Sakuntalam* (The Recognition of Sakuntala). It tells the story of King Dushyanta, who falls in love with a beautiful woman he meets while out hunting. Sakuntala, the heroine, returns his love, but a curse makes the king forget who she is. In order to awaken his memory, Sakuntala needs to return his ring to him.

Unfortunately Sakuntala loses the ring while bathing, and it is swallowed by a fish. After many mishaps a fisherman catches the fish and presents the ring to the king. Dushyanta's memory returns, and the play ends happily.

Kalidasa also wrote two famous long poems, retelling mythical stories of gods

THE CLOUD MESSENGER

Kalidasa's Meghaduta (*The Cloud Messenger*) is a short poem about love, nature, and the Indian landscape. Its subject is a yaksha, a type of spirit, who has angered his lord, Kubera, god of wealth. Kubera exiles the yaksha *for a whole year to central India.*

The poem opens with the yaksha weeping because he misses his new wife, who lives far to the north, in the Himalayas. He fears for her safety, for the rainy season is approaching, when neglected brides were thought to pine away and die. As the seasons change, clouds arrive, charging the mountaintops "like playful elephants." The yaksha speaks to one of the clouds, begging it to take a message of love and comfort to his wife. The poem then describes the rivers, hills, mountains, towns, birds, and animals that the cloud will see on its journey north across half of India.

and heroes. *Kumarasambhava* (The Birth of Kumara) explains how the war god, Kumara, came to be born. *Raghuvamsa* (The Dynasty of Raghu) celebrates the family of Rama, the royal hero of an earlier Indian epic, the *Ramayana.*

▲ *A fifth-century-CE carving of a yaksha, or spirit.*

SEE ALSO

• Gupta Empire • Hinduism • Ramayana

Kassites

The Kassites were a people who spoke an Indo-European language and may have come from the Zagros Mountains in what is now Iran. By 1800 BCE they had settled in a region including Hamadan and Bakhtaran in present-day western Iran, and by the eighteenth century BCE they were present in Babylon, the capital of southern Mesopotamia.

The term Kassite comes from "Kashshu," the name given to this people by the Babylonians. The Kassites called themselves Galzu. Their little-known language is not related to any other known language. However, politically and culturally, the Kassites promoted the use of the Babylonian language. The Kassite dynasty eventually became the longest-ruling dynasty in Babylonian history.

In the third millennium BCE Mesopotamia was a collection of self-ruling city-states. The Hammurabi dynasty united most of Mesopotamia in one huge empire with Babylon as its capital. When the Hittites attacked and destroyed the Hammurabi dynasty in about 1590 BCE, the Kassites took control of this area. Then in about 1475 BCE, the Kassite king Ulam-Buriash defeated the Sealand dynasty of

▼ These ruins of a ziggurat still stand in Dur-Kurigalzu, the Kassite capital in Babylon. The area is now Aqar Quf in modern-day central Iraq.

3500 3000 2500 2000 1500 1000 500 1 500

southern Babylonia and united the whole of Babylonia.

After taking control of Babylon in about 1590, the Kassites established their own rule in the central part of Mesopotamia; the previous rulers, the Hittites, were forced to go to small kingdoms in southern Babylonia; and the city of Babylon was renamed Karduniash.

After the Kassites annexed southern Babylonia, they built a new royal city there called Dur-Kurigalzu (present-day Aqar Quf), named after King Kurigalzu I, who reigned from around 1400 to 1375 BCE. Situated close to Babylon, Dur-Kurigalzu was a relatively small town, compared with Babylon, but it had at least one ziggurat, three temples, and a palace with painted walls.

KASSITES

1800 BCE
The Kassites settle in western Iran.

c. 1590 BCE
The Kassites take over Babylon.

c. 1475 BCE
Kassite king Ulam-Buriash defeats the Sealand dynasty and unites the whole of Babylonia.

1400–1375 BCE
Reign of Kurigalzu I, who builds the capital Dur-Kurigalzu.

1168 BCE
The Elamites put an end to the Kassite Empire.

Kassite Kings

The Kassite kings were military aristocrats who became effective rulers. Over the years Kassite rulers and nobles adopted many old Babylonian customs; some of them even used Babylonian names.

The Kassite kings transformed Babylon into a powerful, respected empire and began a three-hundred-year period of stability and prosperity. Over time the overcrowded cities lost some of their importance, and life became centered around smaller, more peaceful villages. The economy was based on the making of cloth and gold jewelry and on trade with neighboring countries.

◄ *These are remnants of the letter written by the Kassite king Burnaburiash II to the Egyptian pharaoh Naphkhuria in the fourteenth century BCE. The letter, written in cuneiform, is partly a complaint about the smallness of the pharaoh's latest gift.*

FROM A LETTER SENT TO PHARAOH AKHENATEN OF EGYPT BY KING BURNABURIASH II, WHO RULED FROM AROUND 1360 TO 1333 BCE.

To Akhenaten, King of Egypt, my brother, to say: Thus speaks Burnaburiash, King of Babylon, your brother. I am well. To your country, your house, your women, your sons, your ministers, your horses, your chariots—many greetings.

Land Ownership

The king gave large areas of land to Kassite noblemen, officers, and civil servants, who in turn promised to be loyal to him. From the time of King Kurigalzu II, who reigned from around 1332 to 1308 BCE, contracts giving land to the nobles were preserved on boundary stones.

The stones were inscribed with the terms of the contracts, symbols of the gods who protected the deal, and details of the curses that would befall anyone who tried to steal the lands. Copies of the stones, know as *kudurrus*, were erected in temples as a permanent record of the land contracts.

The landowners grew crops, kept cattle, and raised horses for military chariots. The Kassites were probably the first people to breed the horse, an animal they considered sacred.

The End of the Empire

By the twelfth century BCE the Kassite empire was fragmenting, as nobles struggled to take control of each other's lands. Frequent wars with neighboring nations, such as the Assyrians and the Elamites, left the empire very weak. Around 1155 the Elamite king, Shutruk-Nahhunte, conquered Babylon and drove the Kassite dynasty out. However, the Kassite people continued to live in Mesopotamia and even to hold important government posts until the ninth century BCE, after which they lived in the mountains of eastern Iraq and Iran at least until the time of Alexander the Great.

▶ Kudurrus, *public copies of land contracts, were usually carved out of diorite, a hard black stone. This one, begun around 1200 BCE, was left unfinished. Perhaps the owner had lost the grant of his land before the contract was finished.*

WRITING

Kassite scribes used cuneiform to record recipes, legal contracts, works of philosophy, poetry, medical journals, and even scientific literature. Scribes also wrote down warnings about disasters to come.

SEE ALSO

• Assyrians • Babylon • Babylonians
• Elamites • Hittites • Mesopotamia

Knossos

The first Greek civilization, which arose on the narrow, rocky island of Crete, is called the Minoan civilization, after one of its legendary kings, Minos. Crete's fertile soil produced abundant crops of wheat, olive oil, and wine. By trading with other islands the Minoans became rich. By 2000 BCE many fine palaces had been built on the island. Knossos, the biggest and most elaborate city, was probably the capital.

The Painted Palace

The palace at Knossos was a multistory complex built from the local limestone. Halls, staircases, passageways, reception rooms, royal apartments, living quarters, workshops, and storage rooms were grouped around a courtyard two hundred feet (60 m) long. The royal household lived in rooms beautifully decorated with colorful frescoes of dolphins, flying fish, bull leapers, and boxers. This quarter of the palace was positioned in the southeast to catch the cooling mountain breezes in the summer. The palace also had an elaborate sanitation system, powered by a series of cisterns, containing baths, showers, drains, and sewers.

Below the royal apartments was a long corridor that gave access to eighteen long, narrow storerooms. Many of these rooms contained *pithoi*, huge clay jars used to store olive oil, wine, dried fruits, grain, and beans. This produce was collected from the surrounding farms and probably went to feed the army of servants, craftsmen, and administrators who worked at the palace. Clay tablets, written in an early form of Greek, reveal that nearly 4,500 people received rations from these storerooms at the height of the Minoan civilization.

◀ The Bull Portico at Knossos. In the 1920s Sir Arthur Evans began a major restoration of the palace. As a result, visitors are better able to understand what it looked like at the time of the Minoans.

The man best known for his connection with Knossos is the British archaeologist Sir Arthur Evans (1851–1941), who made spectacular finds during his excavations there between 1900 and 1905. However, the man who actually discovered the palace was Minos Kalokairinos, a Cretan businessman. He began digging in 1878 and unearthed the west wing, a throne room, a storeroom, and numerous artifacts. Evans visited Kalokairinos's excavations in 1894 and bought most of Kefala Hill, under which the palace was hidden. Evans went on to achieve fame as the discoverer of Knossos, whereas Kalokairinos has been forgotten.

▶ A fresco at Knossos depicting bull leaping. The men and women who took part in these spectacles risked serious injury or even death.

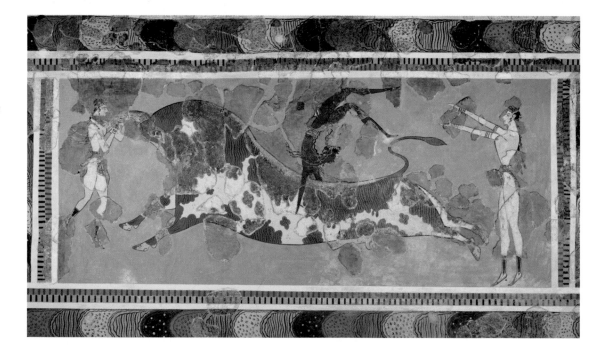

The Minotaur and the Maze

Knossos was also the center of a cult of bull worship. Bulls are honored for their strength and fertility in paintings, carvings, and sculptures throughout the palace. In the large central courtyard young men and women leaped and somersaulted over running bulls. At the end of these ceremonies, the bulls are believed to have been slaughtered.

Another repeated motif found on pillars, walls, vases, and jars at Knossos is the double-headed ax. This ax gave the palace its name, Labyrinth, meaning "house of the double ax." The name of the palace became associated with its maze of corridors, in which the Minotaur (a legendary creature half man and half bull) was thought to have lived.

SEE ALSO

• Greece, Classical

• Greek Mythology • Minoans

Korea

People have lived in Korea for at least thirty thousand years and probably many tens of thousands of years more. Korea gets its name from the Koryo dynasty, which was founded by Wang Kon in 918 CE. Since 1948 Korea has been divided into two countries, North and South Korea, which occupy a peninsula bordering China to the north and Russia to the northeast. Japan lies just 120 miles (192 km) to the east across the waters of the Korea Strait.

Combware Peoples

The first major collection of artifacts found in Korea are four to five thousand years old. They feature a rough type of pottery marked with cut lines, as if a comb had been drawn through the clay. Known for this reason as combware, such pottery has been found at many Stone Age sites in Asia and Europe. Archaeologists believe that the combware-producing peoples of Korea hunted, gathered, and fished for their food. Some other discoveries, notably simple stone plows and sickles, indicate that they farmed as well.

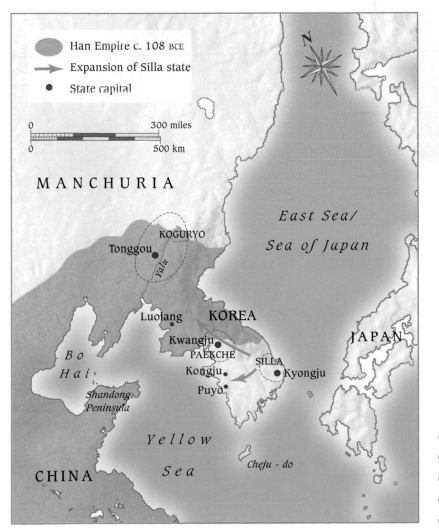

◀ This map of ancient Korea shows the approximate spheres of influence of the three kingdoms in the third century CE.

Rice and Bronze

Archaeological evidence shows that the combware peoples of Korea lived mainly in coastal areas. Over time they started to move inland in order to farm. By 1200 BCE rice provided a major part of Korean peoples' diet. In approximately 1000 BCE bronze tools and weapons appeared. Communities of people grew larger, and many tribal clans and groups formed in different parts of Korea.

The Iron Age

The Iron Age started in Korea between 400 and 300 BCE. Iron tools transformed the way many ancient Korean people lived, making it easier for them to farm and to work stone and wood. Many of the people had previously lived in dugout homes in hillsides and riverbanks. These were now replaced by wooden and stone houses.

The Legend of Tan'gun

According to Korean legend, Prince Hwanung, son of the god who created the world, came down to earth to build a city and teach people 360 "useful arts," including medicine, law, and agriculture. His son, Tan'gun, is said to have founded the first Korean kingdom, Choson, in 2333 BCE and to have ruled personally for over twelve hundred years. Koreans still celebrate October 3rd, the day on which Tan'gun is reputed to have founded their nation.

Tribal Clans and Leagues

Experts believe that the Choson kingdom did exist in the northern part of Korea, but not until the fourth or fifth century BCE and then only for a relatively short time. In China the Han dynasty considered Choson to be a threat. After they had conquered Choson, the Chinese set up military colonies in the northern region, but they were unable to control the numerous tribal groups and clans in the area. Farther south, three tribal leagues, each made up of several groups, were formed during the time of the Han dynasty. These tribal leagues, the Ma-han, Chin-han, and Pyon-han, were collectively known as the Sam Han, or Three Hans.

▶ *Ceramic vessels from the Unified Silla or Koryo dynasties. One of the vases is glazed white, while the other two vessels are coated with a black glaze.*

3500   3000   2500   2000   1500   1000   500   1   500

LEGEND HAS IT THAT PRINCE HWANUNG GAVE A BEAR AND A TIGER THE FOLLOWING TEST:

If you eat this holy mugworth [a wild herb] and garlic and do not see the sunlight for twenty-one days, you will become human beings.

THE BEAR ALONE PASSED THE TEST. SHE LATER BECAME THE MOTHER OF TAN'GUN, LEGENDARY FOUNDER OF THE FIRST KOREAN KINGDOM.

KOREA

3000–2000 BCE
Combware pottery is created throughout Korea.

1200–900 BCE
Rice growing is introduced in Korea.

c. 1000 BCE
Start of Bronze Age in Korea.

c. 400–300 BCE
Start of Iron Age in Korea.

57 BCE–668 CE
The Three Kingdoms period in Korea.

668–935 CE
Reign of the Unified Silla dynasty.

935 CE
Fall of the Silla dynasty and start of the Koryo dynasty's rule.

◀ *This Korean wine vessel, dating from around the seventh century CE, is covered in a white glaze and decorated with a large flower.*

Life and Death in the Three Hans

The peoples in the lands of the Three Hans were rice growers. They used iron tools to plant the rice fields, to make reservoirs to store water, and to dig channels so that water could flow into the fields. They usually wore clothes made of rough, woven hemp cloth. According to scrolls written at the time by Chinese visitors to the area, many people lived in single-room houses made of wooden logs. The wealthier members of society had more impressive houses built of stone and wood.

The people were led by rulers and priests, called *ch'on'gun*, who were responsible for performing religious ceremonies. Priests were also involved in funerals. Some of the dead person's possessions, including live horses and cows, were often buried along with them. In Pyon-han birds' wings were placed in the coffin to help the dead person's soul fly up to the afterlife.

The Three Kingdoms

Over time many tribal clans grouped together in larger and larger bands, eventually forming three kingdoms, Silla, Paekche, and Koguryo. These three kingdoms lasted for over six centuries. Legend has it that Silla was founded first, in 57 BCE, but according to historians, it was the last to develop and grow strong. The first to grow into a powerful kingdom was Koguryo. From 37 BCE onward its fierce warriors repelled the Chinese, conquered neighboring tribes, and expanded its terri-

tory. A group moving south, either from Koguryo or Puyo (a kingdom north of Koguryo) founded the Paekche kingdom in 18 BCE. By 300 CE Paekche dominated the southwest of Korea.

Society in the Three Kingdoms

In all three kingdoms tribal leaders and their families became the aristocrats, enjoying many privileges. The king had absolute power and ruled from the capital city. The rest of the kingdom was divided into large units, called *pu* in Koguryo, *pang* in

▶ *Part of the Pulguk-sa temple complex, first built in 528. This pagoda, called Tabo-tap, is thirty-five feet (10.5 m) high and has four staircases. The ten steps on each staircase symbolize the ten great virtues found in Buddhism.*

Paekche, and *chu* in Silla. Each of these units was regularly visited by the capital's officials and soldiers, who ensured that the people paid their taxes and provided free labor when required.

Chinese Influence in the Three Kingdoms

Of the three kingdoms, Koguryo was the first to have contact with China. By 372 CE a school called T'aehak (Chinese for "great learning") had been established in Koguryo by King Sosurim. Chinese language and philosophy were taught at the school, and Korean officials were trained there in Chinese systems of government. The Chinese method of recording history, its art (especially pottery), the dress of its rulers, and many other aspects of Chinese culture were quickly adopted by Koguryo and Paekche. Eventually the third kingdom, Silla, also began to imitate China.

The Unified Silla Dynasty

Despite many wars and attacks on each other, each of the three kingdoms continued to exist for over half a millennium. The Silla kingdom eventually formed an alliance with China to defeat Paekche and later Koguryo. By the latter part of the seventh century, much of what is known in modern times as Korea was ruled as one large kingdom called the Unified Silla dynasty. Bringing a time of prosperity and great progress in the arts and science, the Unified Silla dynasty lasted more than 250 years.

The rulers of the Unified Silla dynasty tried to turn their kingdom into a smaller version of the Chinese Tang empire (618–907 CE). Korean scholars visited the court of the Tang rulers and studied at Chinese academies. They bought scrolls of Chinese texts and returned to Korea with details of new advances in fashions, science, courtly customs, and the arts. In some fields, such as bronze and gilt working and pottery, Koreans proved quick learners and rapidly outdid their Chinese neighbors.

▲ Built during the Silla dynasty, Chomsongdae Observatory is a bottle-shaped tower made of 365 granite stones, each representing a day of the year.

KWANGGAET'O-WANG
C. 375–413 CE

Kwanggaet'o-wang was a leader of the Koguryo kingdom. He came to power in 391 CE, while still a teenager. He enlarged his kingdom through military conquest, gaining territory in all directions. A monument to Kwanggaet'o still exists at the old Koguryo capital of Kungnae-song. It records that he conquered 64 fortresses and 1,400 towns. At home he promoted Buddhism and built a wealthy and stable kingdom. When he died, the next ruler, King Changsu, built upon his success, and the Koguryo kingdom had a golden age.

SEE ALSO
• China • Houses and Homes

Kushan Empire

In the first century CE the Kushans established an empire including much of northwestern India and present-day Pakistan and Afghanistan. Until the third century the Kushan Empire was one of the four most powerful states of the ancient world, along with Rome, the Parthian Empire of Iran, and China.

The Kushans were originally part of a group of tribes called the Yueh-Chi, from the steppes of central Asia. In 170 BCE the Yueh-Chi were defeated by the Hsiung-Nu and forced to leave their homeland. After traveling a thousand miles southwest, they conquered the Greek kingdom of Bactria and formed five tribal chiefdoms, one of which was called Kuei-shuang. When the Kuei-shuang took overall control, their name was given to the whole group. As the Kuei-Shuang, or Kushans, they then extended their empire southeast into India.

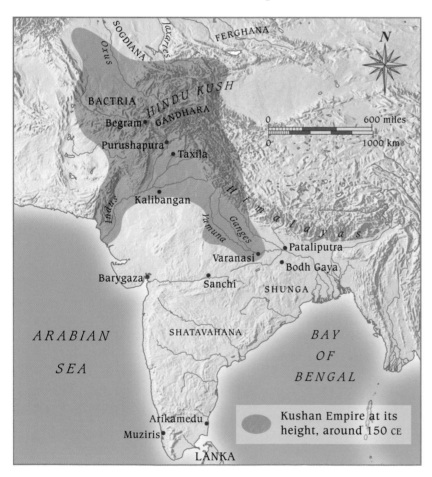

▼ The Kushan Empire at its largest extent, around 150 CE.

Kushan Empire at its height, around 150 CE

Kanishka

The most famous Kushan king was Kanishka, thought to have lived at the end of the first century CE. He ruled the empire from the city of Purushapura (modern Peshawar) but also established important bases in Taxila and Mathura.

Kanishka may have been the first of the Kushans to convert to Buddhism. According to Chinese sources, he was confused by the contradictory teachings he received from Buddhist monks. To learn the truth, he summoned a great council of five hundred leading monks. This meeting, in Kashmir, was the fourth great Buddhist council to be held.

Kanishka had hoped to unite the Buddhists behind one version of the religion. Instead his council created further division by giving birth to a new form of the faith. Previously the goal of Buddhists was for each individual to reach enlightenment and in this way escape from the cycle of death and rebirth. In the new form, called Mahayana Buddhism, there was a different goal—to reach enlightenment but to remain on Earth to help ordinary people move forward.

The End of the Empire

The Kushan Empire ended when a new powerful dynasty appeared in Iran, the Sasanians. In the middle of the third century CE, the Sasanians invaded the Kushan Empire twice, conquering its

THE SILK ROAD

The Kushan Empire sat alongside the Silk Road, the trade route linking China and India with the Parthian and Roman Empires. Eastern goods, such as Chinese silks and Indian spices, traveled west, while glass, amber, and other goods were carried east. By taxing the merchants who passed through their lands, the Kushans grew enormously wealthy.

The Silk Road brought the Kushans into contact with many other peoples who influenced them greatly. Kushan kings used various titles, including the Persian Shahenshahi ("king of kings") and the Roman Caesar. Kushan coins also show different influences. Images included the Greek legendary hero Hercules holding a club and dressed in a lion skin, the Persian god of light, Mithra, and numerous images of the Buddha.

The most important influence was Indian Buddhism. The Kushans converted to Buddhism, building monasteries and sending missionaries along the Silk Road to China.

western half. The remaining eastern half of the empire split up into many small Kushan kingdoms, most of which were taken over by the Guptas in the fourth century.

KUSHAN EMPIRE

c. 170 BCE
The Yueh-Chi, defeated by the Hsiung-Nu, move southwest.

c. 140–35 BCE
The Yueh-Chi conquer Bactria.

c. 30 CE
Kajula Kadphises unites the tribes of the Yueh-Chi and becomes the first of the Kushan kings.

50–75 CE
Kushans invade India.

100–200 CE
Kushan Empire is at its height. Reign of Kanishka (78–102 CE), the greatest Kushan ruler.

224–240 CE
The Sasanians invade Bactria and extend influence to northern India.

◀ This huge headless statue of Kanishka can still be seen at Mathura in modern India.

KUSHAN ART

During Kanishka's reign artists began to carve the first statues of the Buddha in human form. In earlier art the Buddha had only been represented by symbols, such as a wheel, a bo tree, or footsteps. These new statues reflected Mahayana Buddhism's emphasis on the needs of ordinary human beings.

Two different art styles developed in the cities of Gandhara and Mathura. The Gandhara artists were influenced by Greek and Roman sculpture. They presented the Buddha as a handsome youth, like the Greek god Apollo. He has a long face, curling hair, and flowing robes. They also carved scenes from the Buddha's life, decorated in a Roman style with vine leaves and cherubs. Meanwhile, the artists of Mathura invented a style based on Indian traditions. Their Buddha has a round, smiling face, long earlobes and a shaved head or a topknot.

The Mathura artists also carved statues of the Kushan rulers, which were influenced by Parthian royal art. At Mathura there is a life-size statue of Kanishka, dressed like a Parthian king in felt-quilted boots and an ankle-length coat. He grips two enormous weapons, a sword and an object that might be a mace.

▶ *This Kushan statue from Gandhara shows the influence of Greek art. This is Lord Maitreya, the "future Buddha," a figure expected to come to earth one day to bring peace and final enlightenment.*

SEE ALO
- Buddhism
- Gupta Empire
- Sasanians

Languages

It is through language that human beings communicate with each other and express their thoughts. The earliest known writing found by archaeologists dates back to about 3250 BCE, when hieroglyphs were first developed in Egypt, but humans spoke long before they could write. It is impossible to be sure when the grunts of primitive humans first turned into intelligible words, but language is thought to have begun somewhere between 40,000 and 200,000 years ago.

Magical Words

Some anthropologists believe that all languages developed from a single original human language. Others argue that separate communities of early humans developed different languages at the same time. Whatever the answer, language has played a central role in many of the world's religions. The word *hieroglyph* means "sacred carving," and the ancient Egyptians believed that it was Thoth, their ibis-headed god of writing, who gave the gift of language to humans. The Greek word *logos* means "word" or "reason." In John's Gospel in the New Testament, it is used to describe the power that creates the universe: "In the beginning was the Word." Further on, John's Gospel describes Jesus as "the Word made flesh." In Hinduism the sacred syllable *om* is thought to contain the whole process of creation.

Many ancient civilizations believed that language carried magical power, and these beliefs are still present in some religions. For example, in some African religions rhythmic chants are used to cure or curse people, as they were in ancient Egypt millennia ago. In Hinduism the mantra of a particular deity, when correctly repeated, is thought to express the power of the deity itself and can actually induce the creation of a trancelike state.

◄ A painting of the Tower of Babel by Pieter Breughel. According to the Book of Genesis in the Old Testament, when people tried to build a tower that would reach to heaven, God punished their arrogance by scattering them throughout the world and making them speak different languages.

In other cultures words are sometimes thought to have a dangerous power. For example, the full name of Yahweh, the Jewish God, has twenty-seven letters and is unknown to man. Some mystical Jewish sects believe that if ever the full name were spoken, the universe would be destroyed.

Language and Society

Societies and civilizations are defined and united by their language. For example, the people of ancient Athens, Sparta, and Thebes all became known as Greeks because of the language they shared. The Greeks themselves did not distinguish between the different tribes who surrounded them or the different languages those tribes spoke. It is thought that they were all known as barbarians because, to the Greeks, their foreign tongues seemed to make a "bar bar" sound.

Languages may also express the religion of their speakers. Closely linked languages and religions include Hebrew and Judaism and Sanskrit and Hinduism. One of the most important ancient languages was Hittite. Like ancient Greek, the Hittite language spread with political conquest. Both languages belong to the Indo-European family, which includes Sanskrit, a third great ancient language, in which the Hindu scriptures were written.

Language Families

The history of languages can be seen as a family tree. A new branch of the tree splits off when a tribe divides and the two halves develop separate languages. When division is repeated many times, the result is many related languages.

For example, at the end of the twentieth century, there were almost two billion speakers of Indo-European languages. Experts believe that these languages are all descended from a common ancestor. That language, known as Proto-Indo-European, is thought to be that of the Kurgan culture, which was centered west of the Urals between 5000 and 3000 BCE.

Other major language families are the Sino-Tibetan languages of China and South Asia, the Niger Congo languages of sub-Saharan Africa, and the Afro-Asiatic family, whose ancient languages include Akkadian and Amharic. Both Hebrew and Arabic are Afro-Asiatic languages.

In 6500 BCE there were many thousands of languages in the world. Since then, thousands of aboriginal, American Indian, and African languages have been lost forever.

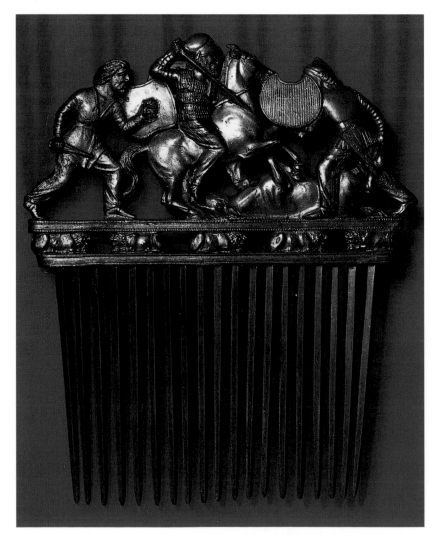

▼ This fourth-century-BCE gold comb is from the area where the Kurgan culture is thought to have flourished. The people of this culture may well have spoken the language from which all Indo-European languages are descended.

American Languages

Experts estimate that there were once over a thousand different languages spoken in the Americas. They are usually classified into three families: North American, South American, and Mesoamerican. There are several important Mesoamerican languages, including the Mayan languages and the Zapotecan languages, spoken by the Monte Albán civilization. Historians do not know whether the Olmecs spoke at all, let alone which language they used. In contrast with Indo-European languages, there is no historical proof that the American languages are all originally descended from the same single language.

▼ *An aboriginal man works on a bark painting of a dreamtime episode as his sons watch. Through art as well as through language, the stories are passed on through the generations.*

STORYTELLING

A part from its role in religion and commerce, language is vital for storytelling. Each society has its own stories, through which it records its history and defines its culture and values. However, the idea of writing stories down in a fixed, permanent form is relatively recent. Many great stories and myths, such as the Greek epics of Homer, the Sumerian epic Gilgamesh, and the aboriginal tales of dreamtime, were passed down by word of mouth for hundreds of years before they were written down.

A lingua franca is an international language used as a means of communication by people whose native languages are different. International languages are especially useful for the purposes of trade. Babylonian Akkadian, an extinct Semitic language, was used as a lingua franca in the Middle East from 3000 BCE, with diplomatic letters between countries written in cuneiform script. It was replaced by Aramaic in 600 BCE. Aramaic was the language spoken in Palestine at the time of Jesus.

The lingua franca of the eastern Mediterranean during the period of the Greek and Roman Empires was Koine (the Greek word for "common"), the language in which the New Testament was written.

Language and History

Languages give historians important clues about the past. For example, the languages spoken in Hawaii, Madagascar, and Indonesia all belong to the Austronesian family. By examining the relationship between these languages, historians can describe migration patterns of settlers who, starting in Taiwan in about 4000 BCE, crossed thousands of miles of ocean in wooden canoes.

By combining linguistic evidence with archaeological evidence, similar conclusions can be drawn about Neolithic migration patterns all over the world, from Bantu civilizations in Africa to the native peoples of North America. Comparisons of languages can be revealing even if the languages are not part of the same family. For instance, the ancient Chinese words for *honey*, *goose*, and *horse* are very close to Indo-European words of the time, and the words for *tiger* and *ivory* are Austro-Asiatic. So historians can be almost certain that the ancient Chinese were trading these goods with their neighbors to the west and to the south.

▶ A Mayan family in modern-day Mexico. Some seventy Mesoamerican languages are now spoken in Central America by around 7,500,000 people.

SEE ALSO
- Akkadians • Babylonians
- Bantu Culture • Egypt • Greece, Classical
- Hittites • Indus Valley • Phoenicians
- Sumer • Writing

Lao-tzu

Lao-tzu was a legendary Chinese thinker who is said to have founded one of the great philosophies of China, Taoism (also spelled Daoism). Although Lao-tzu is supposed to have been born in 604 BCE, no one is sure whether he really existed at all. His name, which is also spelled Laozi, simply means "the grand old master" or "old one."

Few facts are known about the life of Lao-tzu, but there are many legends about him. One story says a shooting star made his mother pregant. She carried Lao-tzu in her womb for the next eighty-one years before eventually giving birth.

Some sources say Lao-tzu worked as a keeper of government records in a state in western China. Others say he lived as a hermit and teacher for 160 years. However, all the legends agree about Lao-tzu's mysterious end. As an old man, he became unhappy about life in China and mounted a buffalo and headed off toward the west, in the direction of Tibet. He disappeared into the distance and was never seen again.

The Book of Lao-tzu

Lao-tzu is said to have written the first book of Taoist thought, called the *Tao Te Ching* (also spelled *Daodejing*). The name means "the book of the way and its power." This slim volume is also called *The Book of Lao-tzu*. It was very influential in ancient China and has since been translated more times than any other book except the Bible.

◄ This eighteenth-century painting shows Lao-tzu seated on his buffalo and accompanied by a follower.

The *Tao Te Ching* is a collection of mysterious sayings that includes both prose and poetry. Lao-tzu is said to have written it just as he was about to leave China on his buffalo. An officer on the frontier asked him to leave a record of his ideas. He agreed, and the *Tao Te Ching* was the result.

Taoist Ideas

The word Tao means "the road" or "the way." It is also seen as the guiding force behind the universe, the creative principle that is contained in all things. The *Tao Te Ching* says the Tao "is the origin of heaven and earth . . . the mother of all things." It continues: "The Tao produces all things and nourishes them. . . . It does all, yet does not boast of it . . . watches over all things, yet does not control them."

Underlying Taoist thinking is the traditional Chinese idea that everything in the universe is subject to two opposite forces, called yin and yang. Yin is predominant in everything that is cool, moist, passive, and female. Yang is hot, dry, active, and male. Lao-tzu believed in the ultimate supremacy of yin over yang. He particularly admired these qualities in water. He said that a contented person is one who never goes to extremes and lives in harmony with nature.

TAOISM BECOMES A RELIGION

*B*etween the fourth and second centuries BCE, Taoist ideas were developed by two Chinese philosophers, Zhuangzi and Zhang Daoling. In the fourth century BCE, the thinker Zhuangzi (also spelled Chuang-tzu) wrote at least some of the important Taoist text, which was compiled as The Book of Zhuangzi.

In the second century BCE the thinker Zhang Daoling (Chang Taoling) helped transform Taoism into a religion. He founded a type of Taoism called the Celestial Masters movement in 143 BCE. In the centuries that followed, Taoism became more complicated and split into many different branches. Each branch had its own rules and ceremonies and even different gods.

Taoism and Confucianism

The two great Chinese philosophies, Taoism and Confucianism, both began in around 500 BCE. This was a troubled time in China. For several centuries the country had no strong king to unite it. Instead China was divided into many small states ruled by princes who often fought one another. In all the confusion Confucianism and Taoism helped to encourage a more peaceful way of life.

Confucianism was founded by the philosopher Confucius, who probably lived from 551 to 479 BCE. Confucius and Lao-tzu are said to have once met and discussed their ideas. However it is unlikely that they would have agreed about very much because the two philosophies take opposite sides on most issues.

Confucius believed that society would run smoothly only if people were guided by moral principles based on family and social relationships. He urged everyone to be dutiful and obedient to authority and to respect older people and traditional ways. In contrast, Taoists rejected laws and moral codes, which they considered to be a cause of discontent and conflict. Confucius thought that rulers should both lead and educate their people, whereas Taoists thought that rulers should interfere as little as possible in the lives of their subjects.

◀ *The Taoist philosopher Zhang Daoling shown seated on a tiger.*

SEE ALSO

- China • Chinese Philosophy
- Confucianism • Religion

Lapita Culture

Around 1000 BCE a people of mainly Southeast Asian origin, known as the Lapita, settled in Pacific islands such as Fiji and Tonga. They were the ancestors of the Polynesians and of many people in coastal Melanesia and Micronesia. From the remains of their distinctive pottery and other artifacts, discovered in more than a hundred scattered sites, it seems that they traveled huge distances across the Pacific Ocean.

▼ This map shows the large distances over which the Lapita managed to travel for a period of more than a millennium.

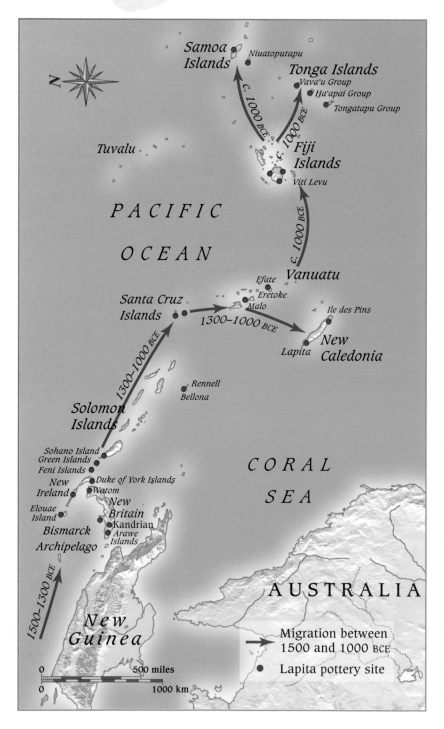

Pacific Travelers

Covering approximately one-third of the entire planet's surface, the Pacific is the largest ocean on earth. Compared with this vast expanse of water, there is little land in total. Apart from the large land masses of Australia and New Guinea, there are thousands of small islands that tend to be grouped together, with huge stretches of ocean between them. Yet somehow the Lapita managed to cross these enormous distances and settle throughout the Pacific, from New Guinea to Fiji (a region known today as Melanesia) before journeying even farther afield. Evidence of Lapita culture has been found as far west as the north coast of New Guinea and to the east on the islands of Tonga and Samoa.

How They Traveled

The Lapita peoples were highly skilled long-distance sea travelers. They traveled in dugout canoes made from the hollowed-out trunks of large trees built up with wooden planks strung together with plant fibers to form a sturdy vessel. These canoes were powered by small sails or paddles.

For their long voyages the Lapita peoples probably used two dugout canoes joined together by a wooden deck, or they may have adapted a single canoe by fitting it with an outrigger. This outrigger, a wooden float attached to the canoe by thin

MYSTERIES OF THE LAPITA

Many mysteries surround the Lapita culture, perhaps none greater than where it first came from. Many experts believe that the ancestors of the Lapita originated somewhere in Southeast Asia, perhaps as far away as Taiwan. The Lapita then traveled throughout much of the Pacific over a period of several hundred years, settling on islands along the way. Others believe that the Lapita were not the only settlers but left their influence and pottery among other peoples whom they met on the many islands they visited.

Further mystery surrounds how the Lapita lived during their long sea journeys and on their arrival at unfamiliar islands. Archaeologists have found hooks made of seashells, an indication that the Lapita fished on their voyages. They are also believed to have carried plants, chickens, pigs, and dogs with them.

LAPITA CULTURE

1500–1300 BCE

The Lapita settle on the Bismarck Islands.

c. 1000–900 BCE

By this time the Lapita have settled on the islands of Fiji, Tonga, and Samoa.

c. 700 BCE

Lapita pottery disappears.

▼ *An outrigger canoe off the coast of Moorea, part of the Society Islands. Outrigger canoes are thought to have changed little from the time of the Lapita.*

wooden poles, increased the canoe's stability in the water and also allowed more cargo to be carried.

No written records remain, so archaeologists and historians can make only educated guesses as to how the Lapita managed their extraordinary journeys. It is believed that knowledge of winds, tides, sea currents, and the movements of stars may have been built up over hundreds of years and passed down from generation to generation. The Lapita may also have noted the different types of birds they saw in order to work out whether land was nearby. Certain birds, including terns and frigate birds, flew out to sea during the daytime but returned to roost on land at night.

▶ This example of Lapita pottery with its simple, repeated patterns, was excavated from the Bismarck Islands.

OBSIDIAN

Obsidian is a type of hard, dark glass, the cooled remains of volcanic lava. It was highly prized in many ancient civilizations because it could be honed to a very sharp edge that cut through wood, vines, and softer stone and rock. It was therefore often used to make spear tips and cutting tools. The Lapita used obsidian themselves and probably traveled long distances to trade it. Scientists have traced much of their obsidian to Kutau, a volcano on the island of New Britain in the Pacific. In Lapita times it was found as far away as Fiji to the east and Borneo in Southeast Asia to the west.

Lapita Pottery

Lapita pottery has been found since the beginning of the twentieth century. Yet it was only from 1952 onward that the pottery got its name and started to be studied seriously. That year saw the first modern archaeological survey and excavations in New Caledonia by Edward Gifford of Berkeley University, assisted by Richard Shutler. They surveyed fifty-three sites and discovered many shards of distinctive Lapita patterned pottery. Lapita pottery is made from a reddish-colored clay mixture. Pots and bowls were decorated elaborately by stamping the clay, often with tooth-shaped patterns. Sometimes a sharp point was used to cut or incise a design into the clay. Designs resembling masks and sea creatures have been found on some pieces of Lapita pottery. Because the style of pottery is very different from that produced by other peoples, archaeologists have been able to trace the movements of the Lapita all over the Pacific.

SEE ALSO
- Melanesian Culture
- Micronesian Culture
- Polynesians
- Ships and Boats

Lascaux

The Dordogne region of southwest France is the location where some of Europe's oldest art has been found. It was created during the last Ice Age, which ended about ten thousand years ago. Paintings, sculptures, and portable objects have been discovered in the area's rock shelters and caves, the most famous of which is Lascaux.

Discovery of Lascaux

On September 12, 1940, four teenage boys were looking for a pet dog that had disappeared down a hole on Lascaux Hill, near the town of Montignac. Widening the hole and pushing homemade lamps inside, they peered into a previously unknown cave and saw that its walls and ceiling were covered with animal images. Experts declared it to be the finest painted cave ever found—a claim that still stands.

The Cave Art of Lascaux

Lascaux is a prehistoric art gallery of around two thousand images (six hundred paintings and fifteen hundred engravings), made about seventeen thousand years ago. The paintings show horses, bison, deer, stags, and aurochs (wild cattle) and a single human image. The engravings are mostly of horses. Besides animals, Lascaux contains painted signs of dots and lines.

Living in the Ice Age

When Lascaux was in use, glaciers and ice sheets covered large parts of the Earth. People survived in the cold and dry Ice Age conditions by following a nomadic lifestyle based on hunting animals and gathering plants. For them, Lascaux was a place to visit, not a place to live, and the cave mouth offered only temporary shelter.

◀ A horse painted on the cave wall at Lascaux. From images such as this, it is possible to tell that Ice Age horses had long, shaggy coats, similar to the coats of present-day Przewalski wild horses.

HOW WERE THE PAINTINGS MADE?

Lascaux's artists used five colors: red, yellow, brown, black, and occasionally white. The colors were made from mineral pigments, especially the oxides of iron and manganese, which occurred as lumps close to the cave. Black also came from charcoal. The pigments were crushed into powders and used wet or dry. If used wet, they were mixed with water, saliva, or urine to form a paste or liquid. Artists applied the colors to the walls using their fingers or brushes made of crushed or chewed vegetable fiber. Sometimes pigment lumps were used like crayons and rubbed straight onto the walls. Another technique, involving blowing or spitting the pigment through a bone tube, created a spray or mist of color.

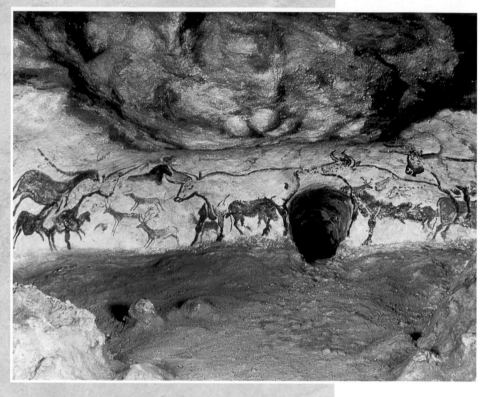

▼ The wild cattle, deer, and other animals at Lascaux were painted in a realistic style by skillful Ice Age artists.

What Do the Images Mean?

Around three hundred Ice Age painted caves and rock shelters have been found in Europe. Many experts have attempted to explain the meaning of the cave paintings. Some favor the idea that the pictures were simply drawn for pleasure. Others believe they were a kind of "hunting magic" and that the images were animals that hunters wanted to catch. Still others see them as fertility magic, where animals were depicted in the hope that they would reproduce and provide food in the future. More recently, there have been suggestions that the paintings, particularly the dot and line signs, represent hunting tallies, records of the number of kills. It has even been said that cave walls acted as maps of the landscape, indicating where to find animals. Perhaps all these theories contain some elements of truth.

SEE ALSO

- Art
- Hunting and Fishing

Libraries

The collection and cataloging of writings were quite common practices in the ancient world. Ancient Egyptian temples had libraries in which texts were stored on papyrus rolls, and Amenhotep III and other pharaohs had similar collections in their palaces.

Digging Up the Past

Nineteenth-century excavations uncovered clay tablets from a huge library created in Nineveh by Ashurbanipal, king of Assyria, in the 600s BCE. The sealed-up caves of Dunhuang in Chinese central Asia were discovered in 1900. One cave contained fourteen thousand Buddhist paper scrolls, collected from about the third century CE onward. In 1947 thousands of scrolls of Jewish literature, some dating from biblical times, were found in caves on the shores of the Dead Sea. Mayan books, many of which were later destroyed by Christian priests, may have been stored in temples.

Private and Public Collections

In ancient Greece there were various individuals, especially writers like Aristotle and Euripides, who owned large collections of writings. In addition, the Greeks also began to develop public libraries. In the sixth century BCE the Athenian tyrant Pisistratus was responsible for creating what has been described as the first public library. There was also a library on the Greek island of Samos. In those times the public visited the library to read texts, not to borrow them. Papyrus rolls were extremely rare and expensive objects in the ancient world and had to remain in safekeeping.

◀ A nineteenth-century woodcut of the fire that burned down the great library of Alexandria in 47 BCE.

THE LIBRARY AT EPHESUS

In 110 CE at Ephesus, in modern-day Turkey, the Roman consul Tiberius Julius Aquila began building a great library in memory of his father. It was finished in 135 CE.

The library was one of the most imposing buildings in Ephesus, with double columns, steps at the entrance, and large windows. Inside there was a large reading area with a very high ceiling and storage space for about twelve thousand handwritten books.

The library was burned to the ground in the third century CE, except for part of the front wall, which was restored in the fourth century CE.

▲ The remains of the library of Celsus in Ephesus, built in the second century CE and burned down about a hundred years later. Only the front wall survived. It was restored soon after the disaster and again reconstructed in the 1970s.

The Museum and Library at Alexandria

Ptolemy I, the ruler of Egypt from 305 to 285 BCE, built his own museum, the Mouseion, to house the famous library at Alexandria. In time about 700,000 manuscripts were collected there. These manuscripts were eventually stored in the Mouseion and in two additional buildings, the Bruchium and the Serapeum.

The Ptolemies were determined to have a copy of every text in existence. To this end, Ptolemy III wrote "to all the kings of the world" to borrow papyri to copy and translate. Even ships in the harbor at Alexandria were raided. Any texts on board had to be surrendered for copying.

Scholars, scientists, artists, and poets were invited to Alexandria's library to do their research at royal expense. For several centuries, through its library and associated educational facilities, Alexandria became the scientific and cultural center of the world. All of the texts stored in Alexandria's library were lost in the late fourth century when the Christian Roman emperor Theodosius ordered the destruction of the Serapeum.

The Roman World

The Romans were enthusiastic about public libraries. A fourth-century-CE document records twenty-eight libraries in Rome. Large private collections of books also existed, partly as a result of military conquest. For instance, there were 62,000 books in the library of the poet Serenus Sammonicus.

Literature

In most ancient civilizations people told stories, sang songs, and chanted poems from memory. Once writing was invented, some "oral literature" became literature in the usual sense of the word. For example, after centuries of being told from memory, the Sumerian story of the hero Gilgamesh was inscribed on clay tablets in about 2000 BCE.

Two great Indian stories, the *Ramayana* and the *Mahabharata*, were finally written down in about the third and sixth centuries BCE, respectively, after centuries of being handed down by word of mouth from one generation to another. In ancient China, India, and Egypt, songs passed on from singer to singer were written down as poems. "Hearing your voice is pomegranate wine," a line from an Egyptian love song, was written down as a poem on a papyrus in around 1300 BCE.

Did Homer Write?

The Greek poet Homer lived between 750 and 650 BCE, around the time when writing was reintroduced to Greece after a dark age. By about 700 BCE his two great stories, the *Iliad* and the *Odyssey*, existed in written form. Homer probably composed these long poems, or epics, in his head, assembling both from many early stories.

Poetry before Prose

Epics such as *Gilgamesh*, the *Iliad*, and the *Mahabharata* were composed in verse, perhaps partly because poetry is easier to remember than prose. Even after they were written down, they were performed from memory, usually with a musical accompaniment. When writing was invented authors began to record their poetry in a permanent form. Even Greek scientists wrote in verse. Hesiod, who was writing in about 700 BCE, composed his farming manual *Works and Days* in verse.

▼ This painting of a scene from the Ramayana *epic depicts Rama hunting the Golden Deer.*

At fifteen I went with the army,
At fourscore I came home.
On the way I met a man from the village,
I asked him who there was at home.
"That over there is your house,
All covered over with trees and bushes."
Rabbits had run in at the dog hole,
Pheasants flew down from the beams of the roof.
In the courtyard was growing some wild grain;
And by the well, some wild mallows.
I'll boil the grain and make porridge,
I'll pluck the mallows and make soup.
Soup and porridge are both cooked,
But there is no one to eat them with.
I went out and looked towards the east,
Tears fell and wetted my clothes.

Religion and Literature

A great deal of ancient literature expressed religious belief and feeling. For instance, early Hebrew religious writing, which became part of the Old Testament, consisted of stories about the creation, history, great people and battles, and songs and hymns to God. In India the holy books of Hinduism were the Vedas, the earliest of which may have been written down around 1200 BCE.

Early Written Literature

In ancient societies literature came to mean works composed with pen or brush on paper, stylus on clay, or chisel in stone. Some early Chinese poetry, for instance, from as far back as about 1000 BCE, was probably composed in writing. The same may be true of some early Japanese poetry, the Indian Vedas, and Egyptian writings.

In Greece some of the first works composed in writing were inscriptions—short poems carved in stone or metal to commemorate a battle or a death. These inscriptions, along with short poems called epigrams, were written from about the mid-seventh century BCE onwards.

▶ A writing tablet from twelfth-century-BCE Mesopotamia, inscribed with the myth of Matra Hasis.

Entertainment and Leisure

One of the last kinds of literature to develop anywhere was prose fiction, which would eventually become the novel. Prose stories had their beginnings in ancient times, perhaps in Egypt. For example, "The Tale of Sinhue," written in about 1950 BCE, derives from the Middle Kingdom (c. 2040–1795 BCE). A second Middle Kingdom papyrus, "The Tale of the Eloquent Peasant," tells the story of a poor man who is robbed and appeals to the authorities for help. In another story a sailor is shipwrecked on a magic island and befriended by a giant serpent. In yet another a prince sets out to find a beautiful princess in a land beyond the Euphrates River. In ancient Greece, too, from the fourth century BCE, animal fables, adventure stories, pirate tales, and romances with heroes and heroines appeared.

Such stories were intended for amusement and relaxation. Apuleius, writing his famous *Metamorphoses*, or *The Golden Ass*, in about 160 CE, says to his readers: "I will stitch together various fables . . . and soothe your ears with a sweet murmuring—provided you are not too snooty to peruse this Egyptian papyrus written on with a sharp Nile-reed pen." This text has been called the world's first novel.

SEE ALSO
- Babylon • China
- Egypt
- Gilgamesh Epic
- Greek Mythology
- Iliad and Odyssey
- Mahabharata
- Mesopotamia
- Odysseus
- Ramayana
- Writing

▼ *This fragment of a relief from a tomb wall, dating from 1300 BCE, shows scribes at work in ancient Egypt.*

Liu Hsiu

Liu Hsiu (6 BCE–57 CE), whose name is also spelled Liu Xiu, was a Chinese nobleman who became emperor of China during the first century CE. He took the throne of China by force during a rebellion but then ruled China wisely for over thirty years.

The Han Dynasty

Each period in Chinese history is named after the dynasty (a line of emperors from the same family) that ruled China at the time in question. Liu Hsiu was a member of the Han dynasty. Han emperors ruled China from 206 BCE to 220 CE. Early on in the Han dynasty, arts and sciences flourished, and China became powerful.

The Han era, which lasted four centuries, was really two separate dynasties, sometimes called the earlier and later Han dynasties. They were separated by a period of fourteen years, between 9 and 22 CE, during which a usurper changed the dynastic name to Xin (or Hsin). In 22 CE Liu Hsiu defeated the Xin and restored the Han dynasty. This victory made him an important figure in China's early history.

The early Han emperors ruled from the city of Chang'an in north-central China. When Liu Hsiu regained the throne, he founded a new capital city, Luoyang, 150 miles (240 km) east of Chang'an. For this reason the first period of Han rule is also called the western Han dynasty, and the second period is called the eastern Han dynasty.

▼ The city of Luoyang, founded by Liu Hsiu, later became an important center for Buddhist art. The statues shown here date from the fifth century CE.

In ancient China there was an old saying: an emperor should "win the country from horseback but not rule from there too." That is, an emperor might take control of China by force but should not rule too strictly afterward. This wise advice was given to the very first Han emperor, Gaozu, around 200 BCE. Liu Hsiu followed it over two hundred years later when he took the throne.

◀ Two coins from the reign of Liu Hsiu.

Rebellion in China

During the later first century BCE the first dynasty of Han emperors started to rule less effectively. Government officials became dishonest, and taxes rose. Finally, in 8 CE, the peasants rebelled against the Han. A nobleman named Wang Mang seized the throne and founded a new dynasty called the Xin.

At first Wang Mang had wide support in China. He tried to help the poor by bringing in new laws, but his reforms did not work well. Law and order broke down, and there was widespread hunger. In 22 CE the peasants rebelled again. They were soon joined by armies of noblemen headed by Liu Hsiu. Wang Mang was killed in battle, and Liu Hsiu became the new emperor.

The New Han Emperor

Although Liu Hsiu was only a distant relative of the last Han ruler, he restored the Han name. Fighting continued for another three years, but in the end Liu Hsiu reunited the country. He spent his reign trying to restore order and prosperity in China.

Liu Hsiu passed new laws to free slaves and prevent female servants from being badly treated. He also ordered a system of dams and canals to be built to water China's farmlands and protect valleys from floods. He punished dishonest officials and supported Chinese arts and learning. Trade flourished, and Luoyang became an important center. By the end of Liu Hsiu's reign, China was as powerful as it had been under the early Han rulers. Liu Hsiu's descendants continued to rule China for another 160 years.

SEE ALSO
• Chang'an • China

Macedonians

The Macedonians believed they were descended from Macedon, one of the sons of Zeus, king of the gods. They spoke Greek, though their dialect was so strange and their accent so strong that other Greeks found it difficult to understand them. The Macedonians also worshiped the same gods as the Greeks, especially honoring Zeus (who represented power), Herakles (bravery), and Asklepios (health).

Macedonia and its People

Ancient Macedonia was a country in the far northeast of Greece with cold winters and hot summers. The climate was more European than Mediterranean, especially in the mountains. However, there was a large Mediterranean coastal plain with a major port, Thessaloniki. Unlike many of the other ancient Greek states, Macedonia had an abundance of fertile land that could easily support its population.

During the fifth century BCE there was rapid cultural and political development in the southern Greek states. This period reached its height with the extraordinary democratic government and artistic achievements of the Athenians.

Meanwhile the Macedonians continued living in chieftain-led tribes, with weak kings whose main interests were the old traditions of drinking, fighting, and hunting. To the other, more advanced Greek states, Macedonia seemed a barbaric place. One reason for the lack of progress in Macedonia was the constant disputing between the Macedonian chiefs. Only gradually did they come to accept the idea of one king ruling over them all.

▼ *Alexander's empire and the empires and kingdoms of his successors.*

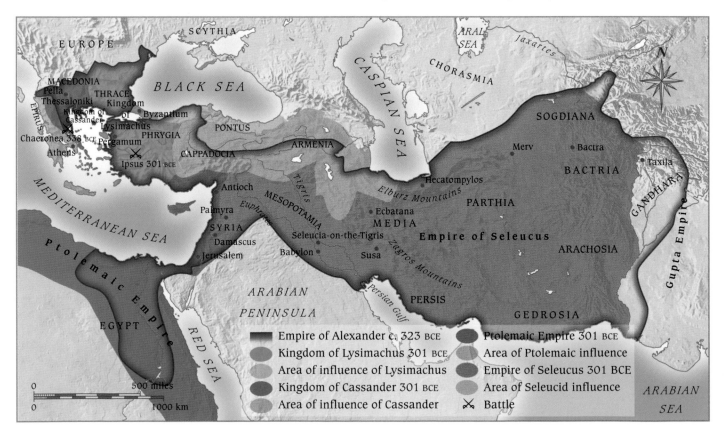

Legend:
- Empire of Alexander c. 323 BCE
- Kingdom of Lysimachus 301 BCE
- Area of influence of Lysimachus
- Kingdom of Cassander 301 BCE
- Area of influence of Cassander
- Ptolemaic Empire 301 BCE
- Area of Ptolemaic influence
- Empire of Seleucus 301 BCE
- Area of Seleucid influence
- ✕ Battle

MACEDONIANS

359 BCE

Philip II becomes king of Macedonia.

338 BCE

Macedonia completes its conquest of Greek city-states.

336 BCE

Philip II is assassinated; Alexander becomes king at the age of twenty.

323 BCE

Alexander dies after conquering a vast empire stretching from Greece to India.

301 BCE

All Alexander's close kin are murdered by this date.

281 BCE

Alexander's empire is divided into three kingdoms: the Macedonian, Persian, and Egyptian.

275 BCE

Greek colonies in southern Italy are overrun by Romans.

146 BCE

Macedonia and the rest of Greece become Roman provinces.

64 BCE

Pompey, a Roman general, conquers the Seleucid Empire (the Persian part of Alexander's empire).

31 BCE

Cleopatra's defeat makes Egypt (the third part of Alexander's empire) a Roman province.

ROYAL TOMB

In 1977 archaeologists discovered a new tomb in the Macedonian royal graveyard at Vergina. In an inner chamber they found fine armor and a gold casket displaying the star symbol of the royal family. The remains inside indicated a man of between forty and fifty years old. When partially reconstructed, the skull seemed to show evidence of a wound causing the loss of an eye—just like the one Philip II is known to have suffered. However some archaeologists believe the remains are those of one of his sons, Philip III, usually called Philip Arrhidaeus.

Philip II

When Philip II came to the throne in 359 BCE, he inherited the problems that had always faced Macedonian kings—warring chiefs inside his country and aggression from stronger states outside.

By 354 BCE, using skillful diplomacy and bribery and a reorganized, retrained army, Philip II had transformed Macedonia into a united, secure country. He then set about conquering the whole of Greece. This goal he achieved over the next sixteen years, winning a final victory over a combined Greek army at the Battle of Chaeronea in 338 BCE.

◄ *This fourth-century-BCE gold casket from the tomb at Vergina is decorated with the star emblem of the Macedonian dynasty.*

Alexander the Great

Philip II's son, Alexander the Great, built on his father's remarkable achievements. Alexander came to the throne at the age of twenty. By the time he died, at the age of thirty-three, he had conquered Egypt and the whole of the vast Persian Empire, even going beyond it into India.

Alexander died in his new capital, Babylon, but his body was buried in one of the many cities he had founded, Alexandria in Egypt. He left an infant son and a half brother to inherit the throne, but his generals took control and soon quarreled in their desire for power.

By 301 BCE Alexander's mother, wife, son, and half brother had all been murdered. After the Battle of Ipsus in the same year, the empire was divided into four parts among Alexander's warring generals: Macedonia, Asia (roughly the area of modern-day Turkey), Persia, and Egypt. Asia was soon conquered by Seleucus, who ruled Persia, and so four became three.

Ptolemy, a Macedonian general, ruled Egypt as king and established a dynasty that was to last some three hundred years, only ending with Cleopatra's defeat and the Roman conquest in 31 BCE.

The Macedonians and Greek Culture

Wherever the victorious Macedonians went, Greek culture followed close behind. This era is known as the Hellenistic period, from Hellas, the Greek name for Greece. The Hellenistic influence lasted in the eastern Mediterranean long into the Roman period, when these lands were no longer controlled by Greeks or Macedonians. For example, although Jesus was crucified by the Romans in the first century CE, the record of his life, preserved in the New Testament, was written entirely in Greek.

Rome and Macedonia

As Rome became one of the strongest powers in the Mediterranean, it was inevitable that there would be a clash between Rome and Macedonia. Rome overran the Greek colonies in Italy in 275 BCE, and the Macedonians later supported Hannibal and the Carthaginians in their struggle with Rome. When Hannibal was defeated in 202 BCE, the Romans turned on the Macedonians, and the two powers were soon at war. As a result of an invasion by the Romans, by 146 BCE Macedonia, whose empire had once stretched from Greece to India, had been reduced to the status of a Roman province.

▼ This Roman copy of an original Greek sculpture of Seleucus I shows him as an apparently kindly and thoughtful ruler rather than a military leader.

SELEUCUS

Seleucus (c. 358–281 BCE) was one of Alexander the Great's generals. After Alexander's death he was put in charge of the vast Persian section of the Macedonian Empire. Though he lost it for a short time, he soon regained control.

At the Battle of Ipsus in 301 BCE, Seleucus won independence from Macedonian authority and set up his own dynasty. Seleucus ensured that Hellenic (Greek) culture continued to spread throughout this huge territory, stretching from the Mediterranean to the borders of India. He was a kindly ruler, and some regard his achievements as second only to those of Alexander.

He was murdered in 281 BCE, while attempting to take over Macedonia itself. His successors held power for more than two hundred years, until they were conquered by the Romans in 64 BCE.

SEE ALSO
- Alexander the Great • Alexandria
- Athens • Cleopatra • Greece, Classical
- Philip II of Macedonia • Tombs

Mahabharata

Known as the great epic of India, the *Mahabharata* is the world's longest poem. It has almost 100,000 couplets (pairs of lines) and is eight times the combined length of the epics of Homer, the *Iliad* and the *Odyssey*. It was written down between 400 BCE and 200 CE but includes the work of generations of earlier poets and storytellers.

The subject of the *Mahabharata* is a family feud over the right to rule the kingdom of the Bharatas, one of the Aryan clans of northern India. The title means "great (story of the) Bharatas." It may be based on memories of an actual ancient war fought over this kingdom.

The feud is between five brothers, the heroic Pandavas, and their hundred cousins, the wicked Kauravas. The trouble begins when Yudisthira, the leading Pandava, is cheated out of his kingdom by his cousin Duryodhana in a dice game. Duryodhana promises to return the kingdom if Yudisthira and his brothers spend twelve years in exile in a forest and a thirteenth year in disguise, without being recognized. Despite many hardships, the brothers manage to pass this test. However, on their return, Duryodhana breaks his word. He says, "I can never live in peace with the Pandavas. I will not give them even as much land as can be pierced by the point of a needle."

Yudisthira decides to fight for his kingdom, although he has misgivings about killing. "War is evil in any form," he says. "To the dead, victory and defeat are the same." This concern with morality runs through the poem.

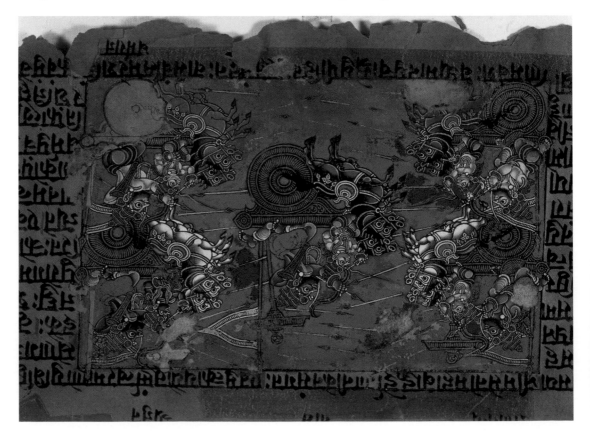

▶ *This painting, from a sixteenth-century copy of the Mahabharata, shows the great battle between the wicked Kauravas and the heroic Pandavas. The leaders fight from chariots.*

The Bhagavad Gita

The *Mahabharata* contains another poem, the Bhagavad Gita ("Lord's Song"), which is one of the holiest Hindu texts, still learned by heart by many Indians. This poem is a long sermon, given by the god Krishna to the hero, Arjuna, who is Yudisthira's brother and the greatest warrior in the *Mahabharata*. Krishna, an avatar (earthly form) of the god Vishnu, has come to earth to drive Arjuna's chariot.

On the eve of the great battle, Arjuna loses the will to fight when he sees his relatives and friends lined up in the enemy ranks. Arjuna tells Krishna that he does not wish to fight them. He has no desire for victory or a kingdom. "What would I do with a kingdom?" he says. "I will not fight!"

Krishna argues that every person must follow the duty of his or her caste, or class. Arjuna belongs to the warrior caste, and so he must fight. Arjuna is eventually persuaded, and he rides into battle.

▲ The Mahabharata is often performed using shadow puppets. Indonesian puppets, like this one, are used in popular performances, which often last all night.

BEFORE THE GREAT BATTLE ARJUNA IS OVERCOME WITH SORROW THAT SO MANY OF HIS RELATIVES WILL DIE. THIS IS KRISHNA'S REPLY:

You sorrow for men who do not need your sorrow....
Wise men do not sorrow for the living or the dead.
As a man throws away his worn-out clothes and takes on new ones,
So can the self throw away its worn-out bodies and enter other new ones.
The self can never be killed in any body, and so you have no need to grieve....
Think also of your duty as a warrior....
If you will not fight this just war, then you will fail in your duty and lose your reputation....
People will talk about your disgrace forever.

BHAGAVAD GITA

HEAVEN AND HELL

At the end of the Mahabharata, *Yudhistra goes to heaven. Here he is shocked to see his enemies, the wicked Kauravas, smiling and happy. When he asks to see his brothers and wife, he is led to the edge of a deep, hot, stinking pit. Yudhistra can hear their cries rising from this pit, which is hell. He says he would rather be with his family in hell than share heaven with his enemies. Immediately a sweet scent fills the air, and the pit vanishes. Yudhistra's family appears, along with all the gods, who smile and welcome him. Yudhistra had passed a final test. As Dharma, god of right behavior, explains, "You saw hell and were not shaken from your truth. Now you are home, and your adventure ends in peace."*

▲ *Kunti, mother of the Pandavas, lies in her bed, in this early-sixteenth-century copy of the poem.*

The battle that follows lasts eighteen days. At the end six million warriors lie dead, including almost all the Kauravas and many of the Pandavas.

After the Battle

Yudisthira is the victor, but he is so sorry at causing all the deaths in the battle that he does not want to be king. His brothers persuade him that it is his duty to ignore his private feelings and rule as a king. Dharma, or religious and moral duty, is the central theme of the whole poem. By fulfilling their dharma, Arjuna and Yudisthira are shown to be serving the gods and upholding eternal law and order.

SEE ALSO
• Aryans • Hinduism
• Indian Philosophy
• Ramayana

Marcus Aurelius

Marcus Aurelius Antoninus Augustus (121–180 CE) was the last Roman emperor of the golden age, a period in which Trajan, Hadrian, Antoninus Pius, and Marcus Aurelius ruled Rome wisely. Unlike earlier Roman emperors, many of whom were selfish, amoral, and extravagant, the emperors of the golden age were dutiful and religious. Marcus Aurelius, though a fair man and a philosopher, spent most of his rule fighting wars at the edges of his empire, in present-day Germany, Iran, Egypt, Spain, and Britain.

Early Life

At the emperor Hadrian's command Marcus Aurelius was adopted by his uncle, the future emperor Antoninus. Chosen to be Antoninus's heir at seventeen, Marcus began his training as the future emperor and quickly became interested in philosophy. He was made consul at the age of nineteen, and in 147 CE he was made an assistant emperor. Finally, in 161, at the age of forty, he became emperor.

The Soldier Emperor

Marcus's adopted brother, Lucius Verus, had also been made an heir to the throne, and so Marcus insisted that the two reign together, although Marcus had greater authority and the support of the Roman people. Early in their reign war broke out against Parthia (in modern Iran). Soldiers were sent east, a move that left the Danubian border vulnerable to attack. Later in his reign Marcus spent many years away from Rome fighting German tribes on the Danube.

In 166 and 167 the troops returned to Rome, bringing the plague with them. It lasted for many years, killing thousands of civilians and soldiers and further weakening Rome's defenses against invading tribes.

▼ Marcus worked hard to improve the empire. He is remembered for his book The Meditations and for the changes he made to the laws of Rome. One of his changes was to reduce the numbers of slaves killed in the games by using actors instead.

> LIKE OTHER STOIC PHILOSOPHERS, MARCUS AURELIUS WROTE ABOUT RULES OF LIFE THAT PEOPLE WERE EXPECTED TO FOLLOW:
>
> *On what then should we exert our efforts? Only this:*
> *correct intentions;*
> *actions carried out in the service of the community;*
> *speech that should never be used to deceive;*
> *an inner disposition that joyfully greets each event like something*
> *necessary and familiar, since it flows from so grand a principle and so*
> *great a source.*
>
> MARCUS AURELIUS, *THE MEDITATIONS*

▼ *To celebrate Marcus's victories against the invading tribes, a great column showing the successes of his campaigns was erected in Rome. It still stands in the Piazza Colonna.*

When Lucius Verus died in 168 or 169, Marcus became sole ruler. In 175 CE a plot was conceived against Marcus. His own wife, Faustina, may have been one of the conspirators, but Marcus loved her very much and forgave her.

In 177 Marcus made his son Commodus joint emperor, and the two returned to the north of the empire to continue the wars with the German tribes. Marcus died while at the front in 180 CE.

When Commodus became emperor, the golden age of Rome came to a disastrous end. He finished the wars with the German tribes, but the rest of his rule was marked by assassinations, official corruption, and increasing signs of insanity on the part of the emperor. He was strangled by a professional wrestler in 192 CE and died without an heir.

The Meditations

Marcus wrote *The Meditations* while he was away from Rome, fighting. The book gives an extraordinary insight into the mind of a philosopher king. His philosophy belonged to the school of Stoicism. He believed that people should accept all things because even the bad is part of the universe.

SEE ALSO
- Hadrian • Roman Philosophy
- Roman Republic and Empire
- Rome, City of

Marduk

Marduk was the chief god of the Babylonians. Originally, he may have been the god of thunderstorms and of the rain that fertilized the fields. As Babylon's power spread over the Fertile Crescent (the area around the Tigris and Euphrates Rivers), he became the most important god in southern Mesopotamia.

Marduk's Family

In Babylonian mythology Marduk was the son of Ea, the god of wisdom, magic, and the underground ocean of sweet waters (called the Apsû). Marduk's companion was Zarpanitum, the goddess of birth.

The Story of Creation

Marduk plays the leading role in *Enuma Elish*, the Babylonian story of creation. In it he is the only god to challenge Tiamat, the goddess of chaos, who wants to take over the Apsû and the rest of the universe. During a battle between the two gods, Marduk catches Tiamat in his net and stuffs the wind down her throat. While the evil goddess is struggling, Marduk pierces her belly with an arrow and divides her body in two. With one half, he makes the earth. With the other, he makes the heavens. Marduk then fills the skies with stars and creates people to put on earth.

Enuma Elish was written down on seven clay tablets by an unknown poet, possibly sometime between the twelfth and ninth centuries BCE. A cylinder seal, found in the temple dedicated to Marduk at Babylon, shows the god holding a curved sword and standing beside his sacred beast, the horned dragon Mushhushshu. The god's tunic is decorated with stars and a sun, symbols that show his connection with the heavens.

◀ *This dragon, the symbol of Marduk, cast in glazed terra-cotta bricks, once decorated the Ishtar gate in Babylon. It was created some time between 604 and 562 BCE.*

Marduk's Wars

The splendor of Babylon was the envy of neighboring peoples, who often attacked the city. In the second half of the thirteenth century BCE, the city came under repeated attack from the Elamites, people who lived in the mountains of present-day Iran. They carried the statue of Marduk away to their royal city of Susa, where they held the statue (hence the god) captive for many years. King Nebuchadrezzar I, who reigned over Babylon from around 1119 to 1098 BCE, organized a counterattack and brought the revered statue of the god back to its home city.

Marduk's reputation in the ancient world was so great that he was worshiped in many countries, including Assyria and Persia. When Babylon was destroyed by Cyrus the Great in 539 BCE, the great military leader insisted on praying to Marduk. The god survived the fall of Babylon and was eventually worshiped as Bel, a name that means simply "lord." It was only with the coming of Christianity that Marduk's power over people's minds finally passed into history, along with that of many other ancient gods.

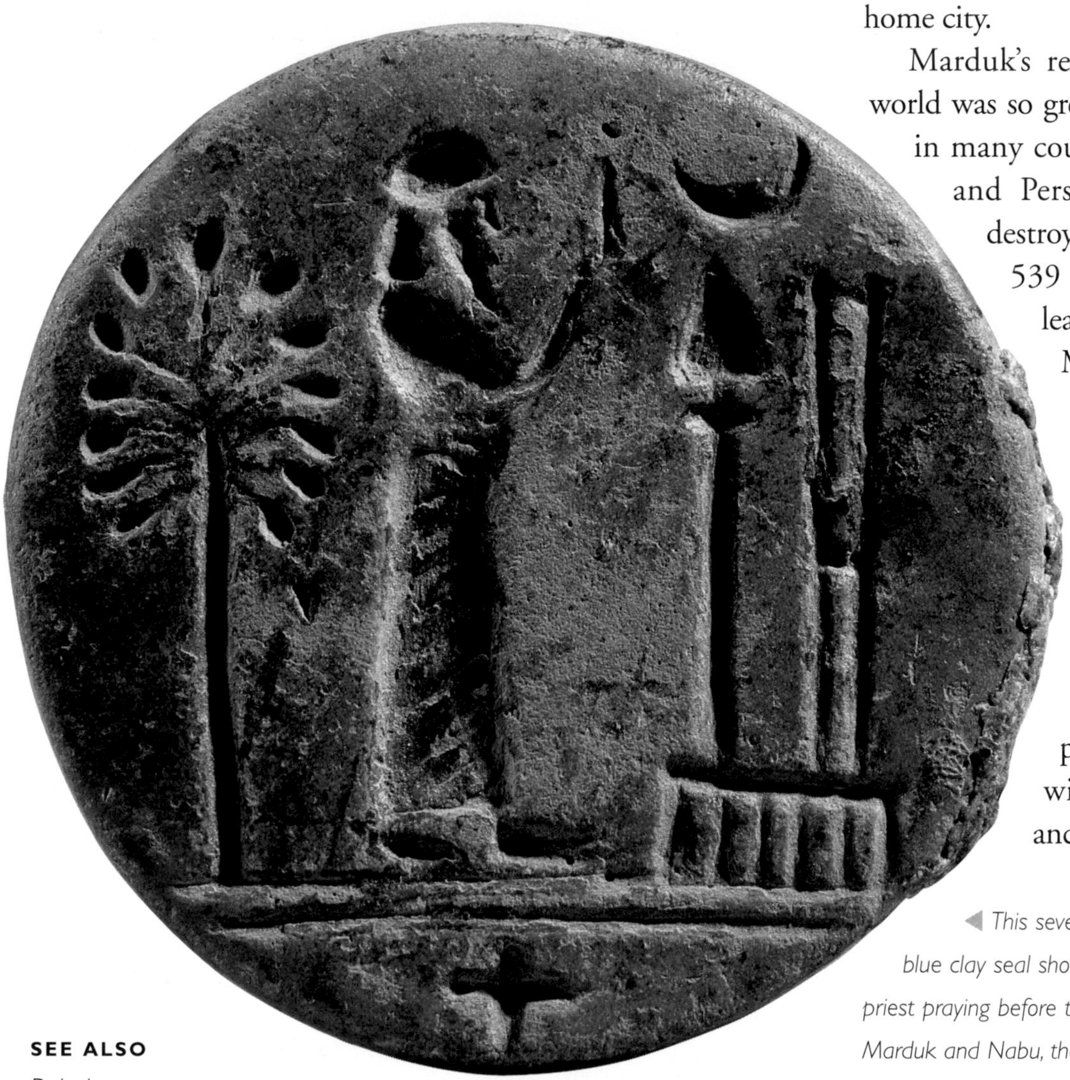

This seventh-century-BCE blue clay seal shows a Babylonian priest praying before the symbols of Marduk and Nabu, the god of wisdom.

SEE ALSO
- Babylon
- Babylonians
- Elamites
- Festivals
- Ishtar
- Kassites
- Mesopotamia
- Mythology
- Nebuchadrezzar II
- Religion

THIS IS PART OF A PRAYER READ TO MARDUK DURING THE ANNUAL BABYLONIAN NEW YEAR FESTIVAL:

O Lord, mighty one who dwells in Ekur [heaven],
Let thine own divine spirit bring thee rest,
O thou who art the hero of the gods,
May the gods of heaven and earth cause thine anger to be appeased . . .

PSALM OF MARDUK

Glossary

avatar Human or animal form of a Hindu god.

bulla A round amulet worn by Roman children until they came of age (boys around sixteen, girls around fourteen or fifteen).

cameo A gem with a design carved in relief, especially one in which the bottom and top layers are different colors. It is the opposite of an intaglio.

caste Class in India, according to the principles of Hinduism, e.g. the Brahmin caste were holy men; the Kshatriyas were warriors; and the Shudras were land-owning farmers or skilled tradesmen.

crucifixion A method of killing used for political rebels in the Roman Empire. The prisoner was nailed or tied to a wooden cross and left to die.

cuneiform A style of writing using wedge-shaped characters, usually made by a reed or other stylus pressed into a tablet of wet clay, which was then hardened in the sun or baked. The term also describes similar writing carved into material such as stone.

dharma According to the principles of Hinduism, one's religious or moral duty.

Essene A member of a Jewish group that lived a life of prayer and fasting in the desert.

fibula An arch-shaped Etruscan or Roman brooch with a long pin. It was used to fasten clothing and hold it in place.

fresco Wall painting where paint is applied to fresh damp plaster.

hieroglyph Symbol in a system of picture writing used by the Egyptians, the Maya, and other ancient civilizations. Individual hieroglyphs could stand for objects, concepts, or sounds.

hunter-gatherer One who lives by hunting animals for their meat and by gathering wild fruits, seeds, and vegetables.

Indo-European A major language group to which most languages in Europe, India, and Iran belong.

intaglio A gem with a design carved into it by engraving; the opposite of a cameo.

lacquer To finish wooden bowls and other containers by painting them with lacquer, liquid sap from the lacquer tree. The artist applies several coats of lacquer which then dry to form a tough, glossy finish.

meditation The practice of training the mind and body to be less active for certain periods, especially in order to focus on religious matters.

Messiah In the Hebrew Bible, an anointed king who will lead the Jews back to the land of Israel and establish justice in the world. Christians believe Jesus was the Messiah prophesied in the Bible.

New Testament For Christians, the second and most important part of the Bible, concerned with Jesus' life and his message of God's justice, love, mercy, and redemption.

Pharisee A member of a Jewish group whose name means "interpreters." The Pharisees interpreted, or made sense of, God's laws, applying them to everyday life. They were forerunners of rabbis.

rabbi In Judaism, a religious leader and teacher.

Sabbath A day of rest, dedicated to God. The Jewish Sabbath lasts from before sunset on Friday until after sunset on Saturday. Sunday is the Christian Sabbath.

Sadducee One of a group of Jewish priests who claimed to be descended from Zadok, the chief priest under King Solomon. They controlled temple worship in Jerusalem and grew very wealthy on offerings brought to the temple.

Sanskrit An ancient Indian language related to most of the languages of Europe, those, that is, that are members of the Indo-European group of languages.

synagogue A Jewish place of worship, from a Greek word for "assembly," or "gathering."

terra-cotta Unglazed reddish-brown hard-baked clay, often used to make pottery objects.

yaksha An Indian spirit; a being, more powerful than a human, who serves a god.

ziggurat English word for *ziqqurratu*, a temple built in the shape of a stepped pyramid, found in Mesopotamian cities.

Index

> Page numbers in **boldface type** refer to main articles.
> Page numbers in *italic type* refer to illustrations.